KEEPING PARROTS

KEEPING PARROTS

Rosemary Low

BLANDFORD PRESS
POOLE·DORSET

615 2219

First published in the U.K. 1985 by Blandford Press,
Link House, West Street, Poole, Dorset BH15 1LL.

Distributed in the United States by
Sterling Publishing Co., Inc.,
2 Park Avenue, New York, N.Y. 10016

British Library Cataloguing in Publication Data

Low, Rosemary
  Keeping parrots.
  1. Parrots
  I. Title
  636.6'865   SF473.P3

ISBN 0 7137 1506 5 *(Hardback edition)*
ISBN 0 7137 1695 9 *(Paperback edition)*

Typeset by Megaron Typesetting, Bournemouth, England.

Printed in Great Britain by R.J. Acford, Chichester

ACKNOWLEDGEMENTS

The author and publisher are grateful to the following for permission to reproduce photographs:

Aquila Photographics: Figures 1 (M. Gilroy), 5, 18, 19 (M. Gilroy), 21 (M. Gilroy), 22 (M. Gilroy), 30;
Cage & Aviary Birds: Figures 4, 17;
Chris Blackwell/C.B. Studios: Figures 23, 24;
R.H. Grantham: Figures 2, 3, 6, 7, 10, 11, 13, 14, 15, 16, 20, 25, 26, 27, 28, 29, 32, 33, 34, 35, 36, 37, 38, 39.

The line drawings were prepared by Miss Anita Lawrence.

INTRODUCTION

It may seem improbable that the purchase of a parrot, or perhaps a pair of Cockatiels, can change someone's life, yet this not infrequently happens. Parrots can be addictive! Their care and breeding becomes a passion which dominates all other interests.

While this is true of many forms of livestock, parrots have a special appeal. It is not only their mimicry which ensures their popularity (many parrots never learn to talk) but their adaptability, the affection which they exhibit towards their human friends, and their intriguing, complex and often amusing personalities.

Whether kept as house pets or in aviaries, members of the parrot family have so much to recommend them. Most species are hardy and long-lived (the potential life span of the larger species equals Man's), most are colourful and many are spectacularly arrayed and include some of the most beautiful of the 8,600 or so species of birds found throughout the world.

There are a number of different aspects which can be pursued by the parrot-keeper. Some enjoy the companionship of a single pet with which a very close relationship can be formed. But for the growing number of parrot breeders, the emphasis is quite different. Rearing young and building up aviary-bred strains is all-important. The aim may be to produce colour mutations in the more commonly kept species, such as Lovebirds and Cockatiels or, when experience has been gained, to breed the more challenging large birds, such as Cockatoos, Macaws and Amazon Parrots.

For others, the realisation that aviculturists can play an important role in the sphere of conservation is an inspiring one. The tropical rain forests and other irreplaceable habitats are being destroyed at an ever-increasing rate. Many parrot species have declined in the wild due to loss of habitat. Building up aviary-bred strains of threatened and endangered species ensures that they continue to survive in captivity – even although insufficient natural habitat remains.

Whatever the motive for keeping members of the parrot family, the result will be the same if they are properly cared for: hours of satisfaction and enjoyment such as can be gained from few other pursuits in life. But mistakes can be made by the unwary and the inexperienced which will mar this enjoyment. The aim of this book is to enable the parrot-keeper to avoid the most common pitfalls and mistakes and to keep his or her birds under conditions which provide satisfaction for parrots and owner.

CONTENTS

1
WHY DO YOU WANT A PARROT?

Parrots have a special appeal: they are popular creatures whose personalities endear them to the human race. For this reason they may be the subject of impulse buying – impulses which can have unfortunate consequences for the bird whose new owner is not fully prepared for the responsibility of ownership.

WOULD YOU MAKE A SUITABLE OWNER?
Before buying a Parrot, Macaw, Cockatoo, Cockatiel, a pair of Lovebirds or Parrakeets, or even an inexpensive Budgerigar, consider the following points:

a) Is your interest in new projects short-lived? If a pet parrot or a pair of parrots in an aviary is likely to be a source of wonder for a brief period and then neglected, look elsewhere for your next diversion. Members of the parrot family are sensitive creatures, responsible to their 'keeper'; they do not appreciate changing hands like so much merchandise.

b) Can you make satisfactory arrangements for the care of your bird/birds when you are away from home? Remember that a parrot is not in the class of pets which can be left in an empty house and administered to by someone who appears daily for 5 minutes. Parrots need constant companionship, either of their own kind or of human beings. Neither can those in aviaries be left unattended for long periods, one reason being that these days they are highly vulnerable to theft.

c) Will the noisy shrieks which most parrots emit disturb neighbours – or even members of your own household?

d) Can you provide suitable accommodation for members of the parrot family? Aviaries and cages are expensive to build or obtain. Can you locate aviaries within sight of the house? This is desirable for security reasons.

e) If you are obtaining parrots for breeding purposes, do you have the necessary expertise of breeding smaller and less expensive species? The cost of even one pair of the larger parrots, plus the substantially built aviary needed to house them, is high. It is therefore foolish to begin with such birds. Experience of the problems encountered in managing and breeding members of the parrot family should be gained with inexpensive and easily-bred birds such as Budgerigars, Lovebirds and Cockatiels.

f) A tame bird should not have to compete for attention with other tame birds. If you already have one tame parrot, do not buy another. Many parrots are capable of demonstrating their intelligence and of expressing emotion in a way that would surprise anyone unfamiliar with them. Not least of the emotions common to them is jealousy. Therefore the ideal situation is one owner, one parrot. A bird's temperament can be completely ruined by jealousy. It can also result in screaming and/or feather-plucking. If the pet-owner cannot resist the temptation to buy attractive parrots, he or she should construct some aviaries and attempt to breed from a few pairs, keeping only a single bird in the house.

If you can answer these questions satisfactorily, the next consideration is the choice of species and, in the case of a pet bird, the even more important factor: the choice of an individual.

CHOOSING AND PURCHASING A PARROT

How does the first-time buyer, with little knowledge and no experience, go about buying a parrot and choosing a bird from perhaps hundreds which are available? If possible, he or she should ask someone with some knowledge of parrots to accompany him, perhaps the owner of a pet bird or a breeder of birds (the species matters not because any breeder can recognise a healthy bird).

The choice of pet-shop, bird-farm or importer should be made with care. Recently established businesses should be avoided; choose one which has been in business for several years and preferably one which (in the UK) is a member of the Pet Trade Association, as unscrupulous traders are not permitted to join this organisation.

Thirdly, read everything you can obtain on the birds you intend to acquire. The best sources of books are libraries and the specialist avicultural booksellers which advertise in the columns of the weekly magazine *Cage and Aviary Birds*. Most bookshops will stock only one or two titles on a subject as specialised as aviculture. A little research will prevent you from making a serious mistake in your first purchase. Such mistakes must have deterred many people from keeping birds when the hobby could have resulted in a lifetime of pleasure.

The most common mistake is the purchase for a pet of an adult bird which will never become tame and which, in fact, is entirely unsuited to cage life.

A large proportion of the complaints made against dealers and pet-shops stem from the fact that adult birds have been passed off as young ones. The buyer is partly to blame because he or she should take the trouble to find out the difference before parting with a large sum of money. In most parrots, the only certain way of distinguishing a young bird is examination of the eye. The iris is generally of an indistinct dark greyish colour in immature birds, as opposed to a much more definite and usually brighter colour in adults. In Grey Parrots, for example, an adult has clear pale yellow eyes; in Amazons they are orange, reddish, reddish brown or, more rarely, dark brown, depending on the species.

The change in iris colouration is a gradual one which occurs over a period of several months. However, few young parrots of the larger species exhibit adult eye colouration before 7 months of age.

In some species, the plumage of immature birds is not as bright as that of adults. For instance, adult Grey Parrots have an entirely scarlet tail (except in the smaller, darker Timneh Grey Parrots), but in immature birds the outer margins of the tail feathers are dark grey. In other species, such as Peach-faced Lovebirds, immature birds are so much duller than adults that there can be no confusion. In sexually dimorphic species (those in which male and female have distinctly different plumage), young birds resemble females. Examples of these groups are Cockatiels and Ringneck Parrakeets. Cockatiels acquire adult plumage at the first moult at about 6 months of age, whereas Ringneck Parrakeets do not attain adult plumage until they are 2 years old. A young Cockatiel has an immature look about it to the trained eye, but even an expert will find it difficult or impossible to distinguish between a female Ringneck and a 2-year-old male which has yet to acquire the neck ring found only in the male.

Purchasers should be wary of a dealer who informs them that a parrot is so many months old. There is no way of accurately determining the age of an imported bird – and (in the UK) very few aviary-bred parrots are sold through dealers or pet-shops. The demand for them is so great that breeders usually have waiting lists for species which make suitable pets.

It is important to obtain a young bird when looking for a pet because even those which are nervous initially will become tame and most will learn to repeat a few words if their owner spends enough time with them. This is not true of adults. Many imported, wild-caught adult birds are so nervous that caging them causes them stress. If such birds do not adjust to close confinement, they should be found a new home in an aviary.

Some young parrots become tame more readily than others; their powers of mimicry are equally unpredictable. However, ultimately it is the patience and sympathy of the owner which will have the greatest influence. It is therefore important that anyone who acquires a young parrot has ample time to devote to it.

Having decided that this is the case, and that all the other necessary requirements can be fulfilled, the intending purchaser should consider the two main sources of supply: the breeder and the dealer.

Breeders produce large numbers of parrakeets and Lovebirds but much smaller quantities of the larger parrots. Therefore, you may have to order the latter weeks or even months in advance of delivery and have a choice of perhaps two or three birds, if any choice at all. However, aviary-bred birds are usually healthy specimens which are easily tamed; many are hand-reared and therefore all the work of taming is by-passed. Hand-reared birds are almost invariably delightfully tame and inquisitive and can be handled by anyone.

In contrast, the disease risk among imported birds is often high, their plumage may be in poor condition and they may be very nervous initially. Aviary-bred parrots generally cost a little more, possibly in the region of 10 per cent more, than imported birds but they are well worth the small extra outlay.

The choice of birds available at a dealer's premises will be much larger than that offered by a breeder – in fact it may prove to be a bewildering choice. Where do you start?

CHARACTERISTICS OF DIFFERENT PARROTS

It must be realised that different groups of parrots have varying characteristics, advantages and disadvantages. A resumé of the most important features of the most readily available parrots is given below.

Grey Parrot *(Psittacus eritbacus)*

Advantages: Superior and unmatched powers of mimicry (among the parrot family – the Greater Hill Mynah, *Gracula religiosa* – surpasses the Grey Parrot in its willingness to 'talk' in front of strangers and often in its ability to mimic faithfully the voices of several different people). Compared with other parrots, Greys are not noisy. Their natural vocabulary consists mainly of pleasant-sounding whistles. These parrots are potentially long-lived, extremely observant and very intelligent.

Disadvantages: Irascible and unreliable temperament; many delight in giving a sly

Figure 1. African Grey Parrots.

Figure 2. Blue-fronted Amazon Parrot.

bite with no warning whatsoever. They are very susceptible to feather-plucking, if bored or neglected or if denied the opportunity to breed. Greys are usually 'one-man' birds: they dote on one member of the family and may not tolerate the attentions of any other. They may show a marked dislike for one particular sex. It is rare to encounter a Grey which can be handled by just anyone, except in the case of young hand-reared birds. The latter invariably make wonderful pets. When buying a Grey, beware the 'growler', a bird (usually adult) which is so nervous, it growls when anyone approaches within a few feet. Months of patience would be required to tame such a bird, and many never become used to close confinement and are suitable only for aviary life.

Amazon Parrots *(Amazona* spp.*)*

Advantages: Adapt well to cage life; some species (e.g. Blue-fronts, Yellow-fronts) have very amusing personalities and are great entertainers, delighting in showing off. They learn to repeat a few words and may acquire quite large vocabularies. They are long-lived; like Grey Parrots their potential life span is approximately the same as that of a human being.

Disadvantages: Very noisy – regular periods of screaming, especially early morning and late afternoon.

Cockatoos *(Cacatua* spp.*)*

Although there are many contented and affectionate pet Cockatoos, generally speaking these birds are not suitable house pets or eventually suffer from the lack of companionship of their own kind.

Advantages: Extreme affection – especially in hand-reared birds – shown towards owner; beauty, intelligence and longevity.

Disadvantages: Very noisy and excitable; the excruciatingly loud screams of the larger species, such as the Moluccan, render them unsuitable as house pets. They are exceptionally demanding birds which will scream or pluck themselves when left alone or neglected. They are also the most destructive of all parrots – even small species such as Goffin's – and must never be allowed out of the cage unsupervised. If they are, they can wreak havoc in a house, effortlessly destroying furniture, doors, ornaments and house-plants.

When buying a Cockatoo, take particular note of its plumage. An incurable feather condition is prevalent in this group of birds, especially in the Lesser Sulphur-crested *(C. sulphurea sulphurea)*. It can be mistaken for feather-plucking – or an unscrupulous dealer may even state that the bird is in a moult. The disease is characterised by feather loss all over the body, including the crest (thereby distinguishing it from feather-plucking), deformed, brittle feathers and overgrown

Figure 3. Goffin's Cockatoo, aged 8 weeks, beside the egg-shells from which he and his sister hatched.

beak and nails, the beak being soft and irregular and breaking easily. It affects young birds, normal feathers being replaced by those with deformed quills, often with blood retained in the feather shaft. Thus far neither the cause nor the cure of this unfortunate condition is known. Many treatments have been tried but to no avail.

Macaws *(Ara* spp.*)*

The large species, such as the Blue and Yellow *(A. ararauna),* seldom prove to be suitable house pets; like the Cockatoos, they are too demanding and eventually become aggressive or pluck themselves as a result of being deprived of the opportunity to breed. The small species, such as the Severe *(A. severa)* and Hahn's *(A. nobilis nobilis)* are much more suitable house pets with equally interesting personalities.

Advantages: Playful and highly intelligent; ability to repeat a few words but cannot be considered accomplished mimics, as a rule.

Disadvantages: Noisy and destructive; tendency to pluck (larger species).

Figure 4. The Scarlet Macaw is not a suitable house pet. It should be kept in an aviary in circumstances which permit breeding.

Figure 5. The Senegal Parrot.

African *Poicephalus* Parrots (e.g. the **Senegal** – *P. senegalus*)

Advantages: Small size, less noisy than the larger parrots; may learn to repeat a few words when obtained young. On no account should adults be purchased for pets.

Disadvantages: Less interesting personalities, generally speaking; destructive.

17

Figure 6. The Cockatiel is one of the most popular and prolific of all parrots in aviculture.

Lovebirds *(Agapornis* spp.*)*

Generally kept in aviaries or cages for breeding, rather than as pets. Hand-reared birds or very young Lovebirds can be tamed for pets. Unless tame, they should be housed in pairs.

Advantages: Easy to care for and, in the case of the Peach-faced *(A. roseicollis)*, free-breeding, even in a cage (similar to the type used for breeding Budgerigars).

Disadvantages: Most Lovebirds, including the Peach-faced, are impossible to sex by outward appearance.

Australian parrakeets

These include the *Neophema* species (Bourke's, Turquoisine, Splendid etc), Rosellas (Golden-mantled, Stanley etc) and Redrump Parrakeet *(Psephotus haematonotus)*, which are kept not as pets but in aviaries for breeding purposes. (With few exceptions, even hand-reared birds are not suitable as pets, as they usually prove very aggressive.)

Asiatic parrakeets

The best known and most easily bred is the Ringneck Parrakeet *(Psittacula krameri)*. Like the Australian parrakeets, confining these active long-tailed birds to a cage is not recommended; they should be considered as aviary birds only.

Lories and lorikeets

These are colourful, captivating birds, ranging in size from that of a Budgerigar to that of a large parrakeet. Their diet, which is largely liquid ('nectar' made up from such items as baby cereal, glucose, malt extract and condensed milk or invalid foods such as Complan), makes it impractical to keep more than one in the house. They are best kept in pairs in outdoor aviaries, and usually nest quite readily.

Cockatiel *(Nymphicus hollandicus)*

This is the perfect bird for cage or aviary, especially for the beginner. When obtained young, they make delightful pets, being easily tamed and learning to repeat a few words. Pairs will breed in cages indoors or in indoor or outdoor aviaries. This species is recommended for the beginner more highly than any other, except the Budgerigar *(Melopsittacus undulatus)*, to which the preceding remarks apply equally. It is necessary to obtain a young bird for best results. These are normally available between April and September in temperate climates. If you decide during the winter months that you would like a pet Cockatiel, be patient and wait for a young bird of the following season. It will be much easier to tame and to teach to talk. While some adults may become tame, their potential in this respect is limited and they are unlikely to learn to mimic.

19

2

EVERYDAY CARE OF
A PET PARROT

Before contemplating the purchase of a parrot, you should ask yourself honestly whether you are a suitable person to keep one. A young or tame bird should not be acquired unless a lot of time can be devoted to it and an untamed adult which does not respond to people should be in an aviary in the company of its own kind.

If you have a strong desire to keep birds but do not have a lot of spare time, you could consider buying a pair of Budgerigars, Cockatiels or Lovebirds. The amount of time devoted to their needs can be small and the birds themselves will be more interested in their mate than in human companionship. It should be remembered that most parrots are highly sociable and, unless tame and totally devoted to their human companions, suffer from being isolated from their own kind.

Two parrots (the word 'parrot' can be used to describe the true Parrots, the short-tailed birds only, or as a collective term for all members of the parrot family – including Budgerigars, Macaws, Cockatoos etc; it is used in the latter sense in this book) kept together are not likely to respond to human attention in the same way as a single bird, or to learn to mimic. However, they provide an interesting opportunity to watch breeding behaviour and, hopefully, they will produce young.

Having decided on a pair or a single bird, and having chosen the species with care, consideration must be given to the important subject of housing (see Chapter 5).

POSITIONING THE CAGE

There is no question about a pet bird being kept in the house. Its cage should be situated in the most lived-in room. Banishing a parrot to an unlived-in room when it is noisy must not be contemplated. Anyone who cannot tolerate the far from tuneful cries which these birds emit should not keep one! The location within the room is also important. If the bird is nervous, hang the cage above eye-level, at least until it has settled down. Place it in an alcove if possible, or in a position where it is protected on two sides; in other words, it should not be possible to walk right round the cage. This will help to increase its sense of security.

If it is not nervous, the location of the cage is of less importance, but it should not be in front of a window or in any other place where it might be at risk from draughts or direct sunlight. If the species you obtain is a good mimic, such as a Grey Parrot, consider that it might be wiser not to keep it in the same room as the telephone. Some birds learn to mimic its ringing so well that it is impossible to distinguish telephone from imitator!

A question often asked is whether it is necessary to cover the cage at night. Under normal circumstances it is not, but if the cage is in a position where the bird could be disturbed by car headlights or other lights, covering the cage is advisable.

SURROUNDING TEMPERATURE

Is central heating harmful? Can parrots be kept in unheated rooms? Central heating is not usually harmful but a dry atmosphere is not good for a bird's plumage. This is easily rectified by spraying it regularly (see p. 25). A room which is heated during the day and in which the temperature falls gradually during the night is perfectly satisfactory; it is sudden and severe temperature fluctuations which should be guarded against. Most parrots are extremely hardy and do not require heated accommodation when acclimatised. Newly imported wild-caught birds, especially young ones, will require a higher temperature than well established birds; thus those bought during the winter must be treated with care.

TAMING YOUR PARROT

Much advice has been offered in the past concerning the best way to tame a parrot, I abhor that suggested by some people which involves the use of gloves. Force should never enter into taming, which should be based on patience and kindness. There are no substitutes! Many parrots (even some tame ones), have a dislike of hands; thus handling them will have the reverse effect to inspiring confidence. Unless a newly acquired parrot is so tame that it craves to be let out of its cage, the golden rule is not to handle it at first. Let it settle down and get used to its strange surroundings and the faces of the members of the family.

Parrots are extremely sensitive birds and many suffer stress at being transported to strange surroundings. Some birds may even refuse all food for the first day. Try to tempt them to eat with a variety of foods in the hope of providing something they find irresistible. Be sure to offer a millet spray as this item falls in the irresistible category for many parrots, from Budgerigars to the largest Cockatoos and Macaws.

If you collect the bird from its previous home, make a point of looking into the cage to see what it has been eating. Also note the position and type of food containers. Some parrots – this is more often the case with those in aviaries – will not descend to the ground to feed. Make sure the food is located in a suitable position (near the end of the perch); also, to start with, place a little on the floor in case this is the preferred food location.

How you proceed once your parrot has settled down (i.e. when it is feeding well and gradually becoming more vocal and lively) will depend on whether or not it is tame initially. A hand-reared bird will be very tame and can be given

Figure 7. Young Budgerigars quickly become tame and make enchanting pets.

some liberty in the room right from the start. Indeed, it will expect this. One must proceed much more slowly with imported birds and with aviary-bred ones which have not had a great deal of contact with people. Whichever category it falls in, talk to it frequently and encourage it to take favoured food items from the hand. Except with a hand-reared bird, no attempt should be made to handle it at this stage.

The next step is to allow the bird, under supervision, to fly around the room. Many parrots are easier to tame outside the cage. They are naturally inquisitive birds and sooner or later their sense of curiosity will result in them approaching their owner who is sitting quietly, eventually landing on head or shoulder. The favoured person should make no sudden movements and resist the temptation to touch the bird. It will quickly gain confidence, eventually coming to its owner's hand to have its head scratched.

If it becomes bold and bites, it should be reprimanded with a firm 'No!' and a light tap on the beak. This is sufficient to train most birds, although some can never be prevented from biting. If this results in the bird being permanently confined to its cage, consideration should be given to finding it a home with a breeder, rather than keeping it caged for the rest of its life.

The initial problem with letting birds out is that they may be reluctant to return to their cage. The new owner may not know how to achieve this without causing the bird stress or perhaps damaging the relationship which is forming between bird and owner. Initially, the bird should be let out at night as the best method of returning a reluctant bird to its cage is to turn out the lights, drop a folded towel over the bird and grasp it firmly. Most birds quickly learn to return of their own accord.

I am assuming that the bird is full-winged. Some newly imported parrots have had their wings clipped and are unable to fly until the new primary feathers grow. Such birds can be let out and will sit on the top of the cage, but if they fall to the ground there is a danger of injury occurring so it may be necessary to confine them to the cage.

Many new parrot-owners enquire about the advisability of clipping a parrot's wings. Preventing flight in this manner is cruel in my opinion. It is true that it prevents the possible escape of the bird, but the parrot-owner must still be ever alert to the dangers of an open door or window. Unfortunately, many escape every year and only a few are returned to their owners, because full-winged parrots are very strong flyers. Generally, they take off at such speed that they are out of sight and have lost their bearings within seconds. The decision whether or not to clip a parrot's wings will be dictated by personal circumstances. In some cases 'Better safe than sorry' may be a wise dictum. Remember, however, that the flight feathers of wing-clipped birds will be moulted once a year and the bird will be capable of flight with only two or three primaries in each wing. The condition of the primaries should therefore be checked regularly. The escape of a tame parrot which has become a cherished member of the family is a heart-breaking experience and one which, unfortunately, is not uncommon. Therefore, every precaution must be taken to avoid such a loss.

Brief mention should be made of the practice of keeping the larger parrots on stands. This is not to be recommended. Most parrots would not stay on a stand unless chained, and this is undesirable and even dangerous. Also, parrots need the climbing exercise provided by a cage, plus the sense of security.

PLAYSTANDS AND PLAYTHINGS

The use of a playstand is a different matter. This can be made of natural twigs with, perhaps, a few safe toys, and provides amusement for a bird when it is let out of its cage. Hopefully the stand will also distract the parrot's attention from the furniture and furnishings.

The safest playthings are twigs and nuts, so provide these in preference to man-made items. A length of chain and a couple of metal rings suspended from the cage roof will keep the larger parrots amused for hours. This is very important. A parrot kept on its own can know great boredom unless its owner

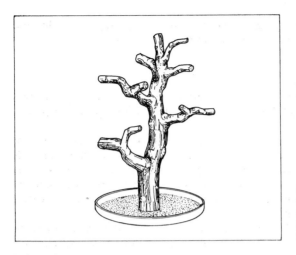

Figure 8. A climbing stand will provide your parrot with entertainment as well as somewhere to perch when out of its cage.

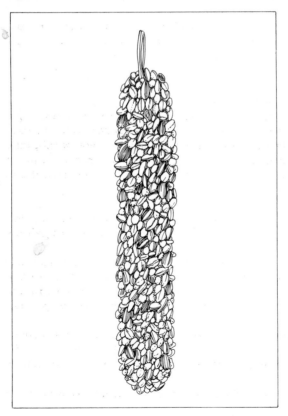

Figure 9. Specially formulated for parrots, these honey seed sticks provide amusement and nourishment. They will occupy pet birds for long periods.

puts a little thought into keeping it occupied. A fresh twig daily is desirable but, in practice, many town-dwellers find this difficult to provide.

CARE OF PLUMAGE

The most common form of unconscious neglect on the part of a parrot-owner is failing to provide the conditions necessary for keeping the plumage in perfect condition.

An item second only in importance to the cage is the spray! A fine mister of the type used for house plants, which can be purchased at hardware stores, is the ideal implement to keep a parrot's plumage in superb condition. The plumage should be sprayed with warm water at least two or three times a week. If the cage has a removable base, remove the tray and base and place the cage over a sink before spraying.

At first spray lightly. When the bird is accustomed to this form of necessary moisture, it can be sprayed heavily and will open its wings in ecstasy, allowing the water to reach every part of its plumage. If the day is a cold one, place the bird in a heated room to dry.

Owners of very tame parrots often take them into the shower with them. The result is a bird with gleaming plumage, which looks forward to this regular ritual.

TEACHING YOUR PARROT TO TALK

When obtaining a parrot for a pet, the emphasis should never be on teaching it to talk. If this is the main attraction, the buyer would do better to obtain a tape-recorder! While most young parrots will learn to imitate a few words, their talent for mimicry is totally unpredictable – some will never learn more than a couple of phrases no matter how much effort is expended on the task. It is as well to be aware of these important factors:

a) You must obtain a young bird and build up its vocabulary from nothing. Parrots which already talk are rarely offered for sale. An adult bird will not normally learn to mimic.

b) You or another member of your family must be prepared to spend much time with your parrot. One which is not happy in human company will not learn to talk. Its relationship with its teacher or teachers must be a good one. Do not expect to teach your bird using only a tape-recorder – it needs the personal contact your presence provides.

c) Do not confuse the birds with several different sayings before it has mastered any of them. Start with one or two very simple phrases. 'Hello' and 'Come on' are ideal because they are short, contain no difficult sounds and are readily learned.

d) When repeating the phrase, exclude distractions such as television and other background noises.

Figure 10. Spraying with warm water about twice weekly is essential for birds caged indoors.

e) Use phrases at the appropriate time. If you say 'Bye bye' only when you go out, the bird will soon associate the phrase with you leaving and will not use it at any other time. When you offer a tit-bit say 'Thank you' as the bird takes it. (I have a Double Yellow-headed Amazon which not only says 'Thank you' at such times, but uses the phrase to ask for certain items of food which he sees being consumed.)

f) Remember that comparatively few species have an aptitude for mimicry beyond two or three phrases. Do not expect your bird to accumulate a vast vocabulary or you may be disappointed.

g) Generally, the best talkers are Grey Parrots and certain (not all) Amazons, i.e. Blue-fronts, the *ochrocephala* subspecies (Yellow-fronts, Double Yellow-heads, Yellow-napes) and the large (and noisy) Mealy Amazon. Few Macaws and Cockatoos acquire an extensive vocabulary. Some small species, especially Budgerigars and Cockatiels, do learn many phrases and make better mimics than many of the larger parrots.

h) Make mimicry a useful exercise. Teach your bird your name and telephone number! If it escapes or is stolen, there is then an irrefutable form of identification.

EGG-LAYING

Mention should be made of egg-laying pet birds. Many female parrots kept in cages regularly lay eggs, despite the fact that they have neither a male nor a nest-box to stimulate breeding condition. A very common mistake on the part of the owner is to remove the eggs as they are laid. This often causes the female to lay such a large number of eggs that her life may be endangered by a calcium deficiency. The eggs should not be removed. Wood shavings or peat should be placed in a corner of the cage and the egg or eggs placed there for the female to brood. She will then lay a clutch of normal size and will incubate for the full period or until she tires of them. This does not matter. She is fulfilling at least one stage of the breeding cycle and emotionally and physically will be in a better condition than if her eggs were removed.

Where persistent layers are concerned, especially those that pluck themselves out of frustration at being unable to breed, consideration should be given to obtaining a mate. Lack of outdoor facilities should not be a deterrent. Almost all species of parrots will breed indoors.

3
CARE OF AVIARY BIRDS

Keeping birds in an outdoor aviary is often the next step from keeping pet birds indoors. Before building an aviary, however, you should consider whether the birds which are to be housed in it will receive adequate attention all the year round. This poses no problems in summer, when (in temperate climates) there are adequate hours of daylight to tend to birds when the working day is over. But in the winter, darkness falls before the working day has ended and dawn breaks after many people have left for their place of work. Unless birds can be inspected twice daily, losses are likely to be high because sick birds deteriorate very rapidly and, if action is not taken at the onset of illness, there is little chance of saving them. The next day is too late.

While it is possible – although not desirable – to feed birds in the dark, it is quite impossible to determine the state of their health while they are roosting. The importance of scrutinising every bird each day, preferably morning and evening, cannot be over-emphasised.

For those who work long hours, an electrically lit birdroom or service passage is almost a necessity. The lighting should be connected to a dimmer so that the birds are not startled by any sudden plunge into darkness when they are away from their roosting area. Small species will also benefit from the use of a night light – a coloured bulb of low wattage (15 watt is ideal). I prefer a blue bulb as this emits enough light to enable a bird which is startled to find its way back to its roosting perch but is dull enough not to disturb it.

When acclimatised, most parrots are completely hardy; thus a heated roosting area in winter is not essential, as it is with many softbills and small seed-eaters. However, ideally provision should be made to heat a couple of shelters for use in abnormal circumstances – e.g. for recently imported or perhaps ageing birds which have less tolerance to cold weather. A ceramic infra-red lamp, used with a reflector, is ideal for this purpose, as it is for nursing sick birds. These lamps are indestructible and have a very long life. They emit heat only and, for livestock, are far superior to the type of infra-red lamp sold for human use.

While most beginners will consider heating and lighting for parrot aviaries to be a luxury rather than an essential, making provision for them at the outset is far easier than installing electricity at a later date.

It is important to ensure that birds roost in a suitable part of the aviary, where they are not too exposed to the elements or vulnerable to predators. If it is possible to persuade birds to enter the shelter just before dusk, this will soon become a habit with many birds which will automatically seek the shelter for roosting purposes. To encourage them, the shelter should contain the highest perch; it must not be dark and thus a wire-netting covered window is advised.

28

Some species, e.g. Lories, Conures and Caiques, will invariably roost in their nest-boxes. These can be placed in the shelter section or in the outside flight. Others, such as some Cockatoos, will insist on roosting in the open and seem none the worse for it. Large parrots are extremely hardy and tolerate cold and damp much better than small species, generally speaking. It is advisable, however, to cover the perch on which they usually roost; a sheet of asbestos or clear plastic on a wooden frame placed on the roof above the perch will provide some degree of protection from rain.

The *Psittacula* parrakeets are notoriously susceptible to frost-bite and should be persuaded to sleep in the shelter where the risk is reduced. The provision of thick perches is sensible as the birds' toes are positioned well forward and therefore mainly covered by the breast feathers.

Losses among newly fledged young birds in severe weather conditions at night can be high. If a storm or abnormal weather conditions seem imminent, it is worth the trouble involved in catching up the young ones at night and returning them to the aviary the following morning. This is also true of birds like Lories which roost in their nests. If the young ones are not able to find their way back to the nest on the first or second nights and the temperature is low, they are likely to die of exposure. This also applies to young of any species which have been plucked by their parents.

If in doubt about the best course of action to take, choose the one which will provide greatest peace of mind! Seeking advice from those with greater experience can be helpful, but remember that you are familiar with the individual birds involved and knowledge of their habits and idiosyncracies may be of greater relevance than someone else's experience.

An essential piece of equipment, obtainable from avicultural suppliers, is a net for catching aviary birds. This should have a well-padded rim; dark-coloured nets are more practical and probably alarm birds less than white ones. If birds of varying sizes are kept, a large and a small net should be obtained. Aim to catch birds in flight. If the net is placed over them while they are clinging to the wire mesh of the aviary, place a towel over the bird, outside the net, hold its head with one hand and disentangle the claws with the other.

It is important to catch up birds as quickly as possible and in a manner which causes little or no stress. This is especially the case when worming has to be carried out (see Chapter 9).

4

CAGES AND AVIARIES

Very, very careful consideration should be given to housing because mistakes are difficult and expensive to correct.

The expense of obtaining or constructing aviaries and cages is an aspect which should be looked into before the first purchase is made. Well made parrot cages of a suitable size are very expensive to purchase. An aviary for a pair of inexpensive parrakeets will cost at least three or four times more than the birds and an average-sized aviary for one pair of large parrots can cost as much as one of the birds.

CAGES

The usual practice is to buy a cage for a pet parrot but, because of the high cost of ready-made aviaries, to construct an aviary or to have a handyman complete this task. However, there are certain advantages to be gained in constructing a cage for a single bird.

Because of the high cost of commercially produced cages, most people tend to buy a cage which is not sufficiently large for the species for which it is intended. The answer is to construct one's own, for a smaller outlay. The result can be a larger cage of a more suitable design than a commercially produced one. The most important dimension of any bird cage is its length. Height is of no importance. Most parrot cages have a square base and are taller than they are wide; in fact they should be wider than they are tall and oblong in shape, to provide an area which will be utilised to the full.

Most pet Amazons, for example, are housed in cages which measure approximately 47 cm (18 in) square and 66 cm (26 in) high. Unless the bird is let out of its cage regularly, it cannot obtain sufficient exercise. It is therefore preferable to construct a cage from welded mesh and metal, or an easily cleaned plastic-coated board, such as Melamine®. A good size would be 91 cm (3 ft) × 61 cm (2 ft) × 47 cm (1½ ft) high. The main part of the cage can be constructed from 2.5 cm (1 in) square welded mesh; only the base need be of a solid material. If necessary, this can be made to order by a metal-working company. The result should be a large, practical cage which will last for many years. One problem with commercially produced cages is that, after some years of use, the tray and the food-pot holders may need renewing but replacements are difficult to obtain.

When buying a parrot cage, choose a shop or dealer with a good range of cages, rather than visiting a local pet-shop which may have only one or two in stock. Avoid tall, narrow cages and buy the largest cage you can afford. It should

Figure 11. A large cage of excellent design, entirely suitable for this Grey Parrot.

be large enough to position a perch above the central one, at an angle, as parrots like to roost at the highest possible point.

Large, beautifully produced (and very expensive) cages are available, designed in a manner to enhance any room. Where the size of the cage is not limited by finance, it is worth making an effort to obtain such a cage.

Perches

The perches in commercially produced cages are made of smooth dowelling. These should be augmented by at least one other consisting of part of a branch at least 2.5 cm (1 in) in diameter for a medium-sized parrot. It should be renewed when the parrot has removed the bark and it has become smooth and slippery. Branches for this purpose can be cut from fruit trees as well as from plane, poplar, elm, willow etc. Ideally, a variety of perch sizes should be made available at different times, so that the bird's grip on the perch alters from time to time. If the bird is kept permanently on shiny dowel perches, sores may develop on the underside of its feet. Rough bark perches are much more beneficial.

Floor covering

The best floor covering for any indoor cage is newspaper. Sand is not practical for parrot cages. Compressed wood shavings (pet litter) are too difficult to keep inside the cage.

Food and water containers

The containers designed for proprietary parrot cages are too small. They can be used in conjunction with larger metal or plastic hook-on containers which can

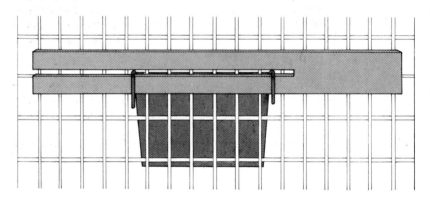

Figure 12. A simple wooden device for preventing mischievous parrots from unhooking their food and water containers.

be obtained from any pet-shop. The only disadvantage of these is that the larger parrots can unhook them with ease! A piece of wood with the centre drilled out for most of its length can be used to prevent these containers from being unhooked.

AVIARIES

Choosing or making a cage is easily accomplished, whereas aviary construction is expensive and time-consuming. It is also full of pitfalls; only experience provides the knowledge which is necessary for good aviary design. The newcomer to parrot-keeping should endeavour to visit several breeders of a few years' standing, study the design of their aviaries and ask them what alterations they would make if they had the chance to build them again. The list is likely to be long!

Materials

Mesh: Welded mesh (e.g. Twilweld®) is the most important component of most aviaries. It is stronger and more durable than wire netting and comes in a range of sizes and gauges. The gauge refers to the thickness of the wire. That in normal use varies from gauge 20 to 12. The former is very fine and suitable only for finches or other small birds but not members of the parrot family; gauge 16 is suitable for most parrots. For destructive birds, such as large Cockatoos, it is necessary to use gauge 12 welded mesh. This comes in sheets whereas the thinner gauges are obtained in rolls.

Sizes of welded mesh generally available are 13 × 13 mm (½ × ½ in), 25 × 13 mm (1 × ½ in), 16 × 16 mm (⅝ × ⅝ in), 19 × 19 mm (¾ × ¾ in) and 25 × 25 mm (1 × 1 in). I would not recommend the latter, or any larger size, because it admits the more dangerous vermin, such as rats and weasels. Welded mesh of 25 × 13 mm (1 × ½ in) readily admits mice; 13 mm (½ in) square excludes adult mice but allows the entry of young ones. Vermin must be excluded if possible because they eat large amounts of seed and are carriers of disease.

Flooring: All aviaries containing seed attract Mice; for this reason the floor must be made of concrete, as Mice and Rats will burrow through an earth floor with ease. Rats will kill birds and may take several in one night; they can create carnage and must be excluded.

If possible, construct the concrete floor on a slight slope with small drainage holes. The floor can then be hosed down regularly, scrubbed clean and disinfected.

Partitions: A mistake which many beginners make when constructing a range of aviaries is to have only a single partition of welded mesh between each flight.

This will suffice for Grass Parrakeets *(Neophema* spp.*)* but for all other parrots the partitions must be double-wired. Failure to do so will result in injuries or fatalities, especially to newly fledged young which are unable to defend themselves from the attacks of adult birds in the next enclosure.

Construction

When constructing aviaries, it is advisable to build them in the form of panels which are joined together. If necessary, they can then be dismantled and erected elsewhere.

Aviary panels can be bought ready-made, including door sections. Usually they are covered with 25×13 mm ($1 \times \frac{1}{2}$ in) welded mesh fixed to 38 mm ($1\frac{1}{2}$ in) square timber. Alternatively, one can construct such panels using an electronic tacker. Easy to use and to load, it will take staples up to 14 mm ($\frac{9}{16}$ in) long. Generally, 12 mm ($\frac{1}{2}$ in) staples are adequate for fixing gauge 19 welded mesh. This method is far quicker than using a hammer and staples.

When joining together two sections of welded mesh, bear in mind that the larger parrots can, with ease, remove the 'C' clips normally used for that purpose. It is safer to lace them with wire and to nail a wooden support along

Figure 13. Parrot aviaries constructed from welded mesh on a wooden framework, with the base of reconstituted York stone.

Figure 14. Range of aviaries for Grass Parrakeets. Perspex is used to cover part of the roof.

the length of the join. It is advisable to cover all wooden surfaces with strips of metal.

The powerful beaks of many species are capable of wreaking havoc in aviaries which have not been carefully designed. The species which create the most serious problems are the Cockatoos which, next to the Woodpeckers, must be the most efficient destroyers of wood in the whole avian order. Gnawing is their favourite occupation and some are quite happy to spend almost the entire day indulging in this activity. On no account should these birds be confined behind 13 mm (½ in) wire netting, because they can crush this with the same ease that they would tear up paper.

Incidentally, Cockatoos and other large parrots are adept at burrowing into the ground unless the floor is of concrete. Most aviaries will need a fully enclosed shelter. The use of brick or reconstituted York stone is recommended for large and destructive birds.

Those who keep Australian parrakeets and Lovebirds will not experience a great deal of trouble from birds gnawing the woodwork, although a certain amount of gnawing is inevitable with parrots of all kinds, especially during the breeding season. Offering branches of fruit trees for this purpose will help to divert the birds' attention from the aviary framework.

Figure 15. Half-depth shelters in a range of parrakeet aviaries; the lower half lifts up to give access for cleaning and feeding. A safety passage of welded mesh prevents birds escaping.

Design

The most convenient form for parrakeet aviaries to take is ranges of flights on either side of a central walkway. The latter should be enclosed completely, preventing the possibility of escape and enabling the door at the end of the central passage to be locked. All doors and feeding hatches should, of course, open on to it. An additional advantage of this design is that feeding can be carried out in reasonable conditions, whatever the weather.

At this point, it is worth emphasising that the only practical method of breeding most members of the parrot family is one pair per aviary. There are exceptions, notably Cockatiels, but the beginner whose interest lies mainly in breeding must realise from the outset that aviaries each containing several pairs of birds are not generally feasible.

There are two basic types of aviaries: those of traditional design which reach to the ground and those made almost entirely of welded mesh which are raised off the ground. The latter are not in general use in Europe but they are very popular in warmer climates, such as the southern States of the USA. However, they are likely to become increasingly popular in Europe for use as indoor accommodation.

The advantages of aviaries raised off the ground are as follows:

a) They are quick, easy and relatively inexpensive to construct.
b) They are more hygienic as droppings and uneaten food cannot accumulate to form a health hazard; waste material falls through the wire mesh base to the ground below where it is easily removed. It is easier to keep parasitic worms under control because the birds cannot reinfest themselves by picking up worm eggs.
c) Vermin cannot take up residence.

The disadvantages are that:

a) Many birds enjoy playing on the ground, scratching and foraging. With a wire mesh base this is impossible.
b) The appearance is generally not attractive. Conventional aviaries can be constructed to blend into the surrounding garden. Suspended aviaries are all too often an eyesore.

It should be noted that, if suspended aviaries are used in temperate climates, such as the UK, a stoutly built shelter must be incorporated into the design to provide adequate cover in cold weather.

It has been said that birds feel more secure in suspended aviaries because it is impossible to enter them. There is no real evidence that this is so. Personally I believe that birds feel more secure in aviaries of conventional design because usually it is not possible to walk right round them, as it is with suspended aviaries.

Feeding hatches: An essential feature of an aviary for parrots is a feeding hatch. (The alternative is to actually enter the aviary.) Many species – not only large ones – become aggressive when breeding and will attack anyone who enters their enclosure. It is therefore most important that food and water can be provided from outside. Ensure that a safe method of securing the hatch is in operation. For exceptionally aggressive or playful birds it may be necessary to place the food and water dishes under a wire cage, with holes above large enough for the birds to insert their heads. This is a safety device to prevent escape.

Nest-boxes: Nest-boxes should also be placed in a position where inspection can be made from outside. When constructing the aviary, bear this in mind and make provision at the outset. Alterations are expensive and difficult to make at a later date. Placing the nest-box in a location where inspection can occur (and the removal of eggs and chicks, if necessary), often makes all the difference between breeding success and failure. Do not underestimate the strength and fury of a parrot whose territory is 'invaded' when it has eggs or young.

There is, of course, nothing to fear from small birds, such as Cockatiels and parrakeets, but in my own aviaries, species as small as Dusky Lories will attack

Figure 16. Nest-box inspection from outside the aviary is essential in the case of large aggressive parrots.

when breeding. Large parrots, such as Amazons, Cockatoos and Macaws, are fearless at such times and they are capable of inflicting serious injury.

The foregoing covers the main points to bear in mind when designing aviaries for parrots. The actual construction is not covered here. It is described in detail in *Aviary Design and Construction* by D.W. Pearce (see p. 93).

Siting an aviary

There are three important points to consider when siting an aviary:

a) It should be in a sheltered location, preferably protected from wind by trees, a fence or a wall.

b) For security reasons, it should be visible from the dwelling house and as close to it as possible. Also for security reasons, a number of aviaries should be located close together, not scattered around the property, as they can then be easily protected by an electronic alarm system. Do not underestimate the chance of theft. Collections of parrots, not necessarily the expensive species, are prime targets for bird thieves. Padlocks, although essential, and enough to prevent casual thieves and mischief by children, are a useless deterrent against the professional thief. Local police will be pleased to advise on security precautions. Alternatively, contact a security company who will quote on various alternatives available.

c) The location should allow for expansion. Few bird keepers will be satisfied with one aviary or even one range of aviaries. When the first aviary is built, the scale of future bird-keeping activities is seldom envisaged. The frequent result is a number of aviaries located at various points, which is not the best way to utilise available space and makes feeding tasks and maintenance more difficult than if the aviaries had been designed at the outset with expansion in mind.

Also, the original aviaries may limit what can be kept in them (e.g. a fine gauge wire will mean that, unless re-wiring is carried out, only weak-billed birds such as species of *Neophema* are suitable; failing to have a double partition of wire between the enclosures because they were built for *Neophema* spp. will have the same result). Initially, most beginners keep quite a wide range of species before finding those which suit them best. Aviaries should therefore be designed as suitable for all the commonly kept species rather than for one particular group.

Take pains to make your aviaries attractive so that they are a credit to you and your neighbourhood. If they are well designed and carefully maintained they will be the focal point of your garden – and even the envy of your neighbours, who may be encouraged to embark on a similar venture.

5

AUSTRALIAN SPECIES FOR THE AVIARY

Don't start too ambitiously! That is the best advice which can be offered to the beginner with an aviary. Gain your knowledge of aviculture (breeding the non-domesticated species of birds) with relatively inexpensive and free-breeding subjects.

All the species in the lower price range are suitable for the beginner: they are low-priced because they are prolific and because they are aviary-bred, not imported. The species in this group are Cockatiels, Peach-faced Lovebirds, Indian Ring-necked Parrakeets and certain Australian parrakeets, notably Bourke's and Turquoisine Grass Parrakeets, Redrumps and Golden-mantled Rosellas. For the first couple of years at least, it is advisable to confine your collection to these species. They are easily obtainable, hardy (with the possible exception of Turquoisines) and, with a little luck, will produce young in their second or third year.

A start should be made with young birds: they have many advantages. One point in their favour, which seldom seems to be considered, is that it is easier to form compatible pairs using young birds which have not previously been mated. For breeding purposes, young birds are a lesser risk. With adult birds, there is always the possibility that they have been sold because they failed to breed or had some vice, such as egg-eating or feather-plucking their young or, more seriously with some males (especially with the larger species), that they have killed a female.

Another point in favour of young birds is that they settle down more readily under new management than do adults. It is also a fact, verified by a leading veterinarian, who carries out many autopsies on parrots, that numerous adult birds die shortly after removal to a new home. The only reason that can be found is stress. Also, it is a simple matter to persuade young birds to sample new foods. Most breeders have their special rearing foods which an adult bird from an outside source may refuse to eat. Where potential breeding birds are concerned, this can make all the difference in the quality of the chicks they will rear.

The main disadvantage of buying young birds is that in some species, Cockatiels for example, it is not possible to sex them with certainty until after the first moult. However, even then they are young enough to be untried and to settle down well in a new home.

The best source of all the species mentioned above is the breeder, who can tell you the idiosyncracies of the birds you buy and advise you on how to feed and care for them. Breeders are usually only too pleased to advise on any problems which may arise after purchase. Many dealers do not have the necessary knowledge to do this. Also, their stock is likely to be more expensive than that offered by a breeder.

There is a golden rule in breeding parrots: one pair to each aviary. Of course there is an exception to every rule and, in this case, that exception is the Cockatiel *(Nymphicus hollandicus)*. Most Cockatiels are gentle birds and can be kept on the colony system (i.e. several pairs in one enclosure), or a single pair can be housed in an aviary containing Finches and other seed-eaters. This fact is important to beginners, most of whom start with mixed collections.

COCKATIEL

The Cockatiel is undoubtedly responsible for more recruits to the hobby of breeding parrots than any other bird. Deservedly, it has attained a popularity which is surpassed only by the long-domesticated Budgerigar and Canary. It, too, can be considered as a domesticated species, for no wild-caught Cockatiels have reached Europe since before 1960.

It has many attributes: beauty, a friendly and pleasing personality, a great willingness to reproduce and – a point which is seldom mentioned – a great potential for longevity. Probably the oldest Cockatiel reported to date was the one hatched in 1932 which died in Houston, Texas, in 1972. The female of a pair in my possession died when she was 28 years old; the male is 30 years old and still active and whistling and talking.

As well as being a suitable stepping stone from Budgerigars to larger species, Cockatiels can be recommended for those with no previous experience of keeping birds. During the past 20 years, an increasing range of colours and mutations has been bred. The original colour, the Grey (Normal), is the most common and inexpensive. It is mainly grey, darker above, with a large white patch extending almost the entire length of the wing, yellow face, bright orange cheek patches and yellow and grey crest. The crest provides a clue to the fact that this is actually a member of the Cockatoo family, although its long tail may mislead beginners into believing that it is a parrakeet.

Adult Normal Cockatiels are easy to sex. The underside of the tail is black in the male and barred with grey and yellow in the female. Before the first moult, young males are indistinguishable from adult females, except for their shorter tails.

The next most numerous colour is the mainly white bird with orange cheeks, which may or may not be suffused overall with yellow. Confusingly to the beginner, this mutation is known variously as White, Lutino or Albino. Sexing is less obvious; however, close examination of the underside of the tail and flight feathers of adults will reveal that these are faintly barred with yellow in females and pure white in males. The barred markings are found in all young birds.

The Pied mutation is a handsome one which is likely to attract beginners. Large areas of white replace the grey plumage. The only reliable guide to sex in this mutation is behaviour – more specifically song. Young Cockatiels usually commence to warble when between 7 and 9 weeks old. Hens do so for a short period only, perhaps only for 3 weeks, while in males the warbling always persists.

Figure 17. The Pied is among the most popular of the Cockatiel mutations.

If young Pieds are ringed with split rings of various colours, a note can be made of their sex as soon as this becomes apparent.

The other mutations are more expensive and should not be obtained for breeding purposes until experience has been gained with the better known ones. They include the Pearl, in which many of the feathers are margined with white (males lose their markings, usually at the first moult, sometimes later), Cinnamon (light brownish grey compared with the grey of the Normal) and White-faced (lacking the orange cheek markings). For those interested in genetics, the breeding of composite mutations (such as Cinnamon Pearl Pied) is a challenge.

Cockatiels will breed in indoor or outdoor flights or even in cages. The minimum-sized cage for a breeding pair should be 120 cm (4 ft) long × 61 cm (2 ft) wide and 61 cm (2 ft) high. Most breeders prefer to give their birds more space and use flights at least 240 cm (8 ft) long, 61 or 91 cm (2 or 3 ft) wide and 180 cm (6 ft) high for each pair. If breeding from three or four pairs on the colony system, all the birds should be placed in the aviary at the same time and must include even numbers of males and females. Any trouble-makers should be removed but even numbers of both sexes should always be left in the aviary. An aviary for three pairs should measure in the region of 300 cm (10 ft) long, 180 cm (6 ft) wide and 180 cm (6 ft) high to allow for the increased population when the young fledge.

When colony-breeding, whatever the species, disruptions do occur at breeding time – perhaps fights over females, hens entering each other's nest-boxes or newly fledged young being attacked by adults other than their parents. Generally, colony-breeding is less successful than providing each pair with a separate enclosure. It is therefore worth considering an aviary which can be divided by partitions during the breeding season; the partitions can be removed to allow all the birds to fly together in a larger space during the winter. Such an aviary for three pairs could measure 270 cm (9 ft) square, each pair occupying a flight 270 cm (9 ft) long and 91 cm (3 ft) wide.

Initially, the great advantage of this system is that, on introduction to the aviary, preferably simultaneously, the birds can choose their own partners. The importance of compatibility must never be underestimated – and Cockatiels often show marked preferences, sometimes refusing to pair with the partner provided. When the birds have paired up to their liking, the partitions can be erected and the pairs placed in their enclosures for breeding, preferably several weeks in advance.

Cockatiels are ready nesters and few birds over 10 months old will not make an attempt to nest. There is a good demand for young birds for pets so, with a little luck, the beginner will have some return for the financial outlay and a tremendous amount of satisfaction from watching the breeding cycle and eventual emergence of the young.

Nest-boxes can be introduced in March or April, depending on the weather conditions and the location. A suitable size for Cockatiels is 31 to 38 cm (12 to 15 in) high and 23 cm (9 in) square. The entrance hole should be about 6 cm (2½ in) in diameter. A clutch will consist of four, five or more eggs. These are incubated by male and female (the male doing most of the incubation during the daylight hours) for about 19 days, a little longer on occasions. Incubation may not commence until the second egg has been laid, which means that the first two chicks should hatch simultaneously. Newly hatched chicks are covered in bright yellow down. Red-eyed birds such as Albinos can be distinguished from black-eyed young on hatching, as the eye colour is discernible under the skin.

Both parents share the task of rearing the young, which leave the nest when aged between 4 and 5 weeks. The female will lay the eggs of her second clutch shortly after, or perhaps even before, the last youngster has left the nest. During this period, the young will solicit food from their parents, especially from the male, by bobbing the head up and down and making a whining sound. Within a few days, they will have started to feed on their own but should be left with their parents for 2 or 3 weeks after leaving the nest. They can be left for a longer period as Cockatiels do not normally show aggression towards their young, but if they are destined for pets, they should go to their new home or be caged indoors as soon as possible.

AUSTRALIAN PARRAKEETS

In common with other Australian species, there have been no commercial importations of Australian parrakeets for over 20 years. Fortunately, most Australian parrakeets adapt well to captivity and have been aviary-bred for many generations. In the wild, most species are ground-feeders, and seeds form the main item of their diet, unlike that of most parrots. They are, therefore, ideal subjects for domestication because in captivity too, seed provides the mainstay of their diet.

Australian parrakeets are wisely included in the initial choice of nearly all breeders of parrots. Many will never look any further.

Golden-mantled Rosella

An exceptionally handsome bird, which is very reasonably priced and easily obtainable, is the Golden-mantled Rosella Parrakeet. Brilliantly coloured, it is the

Figure 18. The Golden-mantled or Eastern Rosella *(Platycercus elegans)*.

epitome of a tropical species. The head is scarlet with a white cheek patch, the wing feathers are black, broadly margined with yellow, and the long tail is green, blue and white. The overall length is 30 cm (12 in). This species can be difficult to sex, as some females are as brightly coloured as males. Usually, however, females have brownish grey feathers surrounding the eyes and these are not present in the male. Generally there is a difference in the shape of the head, that of the male having more height above the eye; the head and bill tend to be larger than in the female. Immature birds differ from the female in having the nape and hindcrown green, not red.

It should be realised from the outset that Rosellas are aggressive birds which are not suitable companions for other species. Each pair should have its own enclosure. Also males can behave quite viciously towards females, especially when first introduced. The male should be observed carefully for any signs of incompatibility. If he persecutes the female, the flight feathers on one wing should be cut so that the female can escape his unwelcome attention.

Rosellas, like Cockatiels, have a long breeding life, starting at the age of 1 or 2 years and extending into the 20s, with luck. They lay five to eight eggs and sometimes prove double-brooded, so a good pair can be extremely prolific. However, it would be a mistake to buy any species for this reason, calculating how much profit one can make in a season, because, in practice, it is seldom that easy!

Redrump Parrakeet

The Redrump Parrakeet *(Psephotus haematonotus)* is another Australian species which is invariably recommended for the beginner. It has an important advantage over the Rosella: it is very easy to sex. The red rump which gives the bird its name is found only in the male. It is otherwise mainly green, brightest on the head and breast. Vent and undertail coverts are white. Tail feathers are green, tinged with blue, the outer ones being tipped with white. The bill is grey. The length is 27 cm (10½ in).

The female has no bright colours. She is greyish green above and yellowish olive green below; wing coverts are pale blue and the rump is green. Young birds can be sexed even before they leave the nest by the rump colour: males have some red on the rump.

A popular mutation is that in which all the colours are paler (dilute): it is known as the Yellow Redrump – a misleading name since the plumage is not bright yellow but suffused with greenish grey. Females are a creamy buff colour.

Redrumps have several important advantages, as well as being easy to sex. Their voices are quite pleasant and will not annoy neighbours who would object to noisier parrakeets (such as the Princess of Wales Parrakeet) and, above all, they make wonderful foster parents and will rear the young of species which differ greatly from themselves.

Four to six is the normal clutch size of the Redrump Parrakeet. The incubation period is about 19 days and usually commences with the laying of the second egg. The young spend about 30 days in the nest. When they emerge, the behaviour of the adult male must be closely observed as some males will attack or kill their male offspring.

Grass Parrakeets

Small, quiet and very prettily coloured, the Grass Parrakeets *(Neophema* spp.*)* are such favourites with some breeders that they keep nothing else.

Two points should be borne in mind when housing species of *Neophema*: they are not destructive to wood or wire and can be kept in wire-netting aviaries (rather than those constructed of the stronger welded mesh); they have a lower tolerance to cold damp winter weather than the larger parrakeets and must have a shelter in which they can be confined in damp weather. Alternatively, their flights can be built onto a birdroom.

Seeding grasses being a favourite and natural food of these small parrakeets, turf floors might seem to be a good idea. In practice, however, they do not prove practical for small aviaries. Instead, grass seed can be planted in boxes or trays and replaced frequently.

A question often asked by beginners is which parrakeets can be kept with Finches and other small seed-eaters. Few can be recommended as few can be trusted with smaller birds. The *Neophema* parrakeets are the exception – apart from, possibly, the Turquoisine. The others are gentle – so gentle in fact that the problem which arises under these circumstances is preventing Finches from taking over the larger birds' nests! Several parrakeet nest-boxes should therefore be available.

The initial appeal of these birds is undoubtedly their exquisite plumage but they have another important point in their favour – they are free-breeding. Two of the seven members of this genus are virtually unknown in captivity. In order of popularity, the Bourke's *(N. bourkii)* and Turquoisine *(N. pulchella)* come first, followed by the Splendid *(N. splendida)*, the Elegant *(N. elegans)* and the Blue-winged *(N. chrysostoma)*.

Bourke's Parrakeet: The Bourke's colouration is a complete contrast to that of the other members of the genus, which are mainly green. Indeed, its plumage is among the most distinctive of all parrakeets, being shades of brown, pink and blue. The upper parts are brownish with buff margins to the wing coverts and some violet in the wings. The brown feathers of face and breast are margined with pink and the abdomen is pink in the male, less bright in the female, whose pink feathers are marked with buff. Usually the male's forehead is blue, while the female lacks this colour. Overall, there is considerable variation in individuals; the best are extremely beautiful so the breeder should be selective in the birds retained for breeding purposes. Mutations have been established but they have not proved free-breeding and remain expensive.

The length of this species and of the other species of *Neophema* is 20 cm (8 in). Immature Bourke's have little pink on the abdomen; some males have a few blue feathers on the forehead.

The Bourke's has so many attributes that it can be considered an ideal beginner's bird. One advantage is that it can be kept in a mixed collection with small birds such as Finches; another is its gentle and confiding character. Unlike most parrots, it is habitually active at dusk; an indication of its crepuscular habits is provided by the large dark eyes.

This species, like the other *Neophema* species mentioned here, lays four or five eggs which are incubated by the female for 18 or 19 days. On hatching, chicks are covered with white down. They stay in the nest for 4 to 4½ weeks.

Turquoisine and Splendid Parrakeets: Two species which may be confused – especially the females – are the Turquoisine and the Splendid. The males are easily distinguished as the Turquoisine has a dark red patch extending down the wing. Female Turquoisines differ from female Splendids in having less blue on the head and face; the blue is confined to the top of the head and small areas above and

Figure 19. The Turquoisine Parrakeet.

below the eyes; the lores are white, not blue as in the female Splendid. The blue is a slightly deeper shade in the Turquoisine.

The face and upper wing coverts of the male Turquoisine are a brilliant turquoise, whereas the upper parts are green and the underparts yellow. The female is duller throughout and lacks the red wing patch.

Both these species need to be seen in the flesh, as no written description can do justice to their glowing colours. The Splendid is undoubtedly one of the most brilliantly coloured birds in existence, yet it is relatively inexpensive and easily cared for. The almost luminous quality of the blue on the throat and cheeks is striking and unusual, a contrast to the blue of the rest of the head. The wing feathers are light and dark blue and the underparts are yellow with the breast scarlet. The upper parts and the tail are green. The female has no red on the breast.

Personalities of the two species differ greatly. Turquoisines can be quite aggressive towards their females and towards other birds, while Splendids are more gentle.

For those interested in mutations, both species represent a challenge, with one established mutation which has not proved free-breeding. The Yellow Turquoisine is a beautiful bird (black-eyed, yellow plumage with the blue areas retained) while the Blue Splendid is an unusual study in delicate tones. The shade of blue varies in individuals, being greenish blue in some. The colour on the cock's chest can vary from pinkish apricot to orange. Females have blue chests, blue or bluish green backs and cream or white underparts. Difficult to breed, this mutation is not

Figure 20. Quiet, pretty and not destructive, the Elegant Grass Parrakeet is an ideal aviary bird.

recommended for the beginner at the present time. Further mutations are certain to be established in the coming years.

Elegant Grass Parrakeet: Of slimmer build and more subtle colouration is the Elegant Grass Parrakeet *(N. elegans)*. It is recognised by the head coloration: a frontal band of dark blue, followed by a narrower line of light blue extending to the eye. The male has the crown and upper parts a rich golden olive, usually with an orange patch on the abdomen; the female lacks these characteristics. Immature birds lack the frontal band but otherwise resemble the female.

Blue-winged Grass Parrakeet: The most neglected *Neophema* available is the Blue-winged Grass Parrakeet *(N. chrysostoma)* which can be recommended to the beginner because it is hardy, inoffensive and deserves more devotees. Similar to the Elegant in many respects, it can be distinguished by its more robust build and greener shade on the underparts. In the double frontal band of dark blue and paler blue, the latter does not extend as far as the eye. The wing coverts are a deeper blue and the area is more extensive than in the Elegant. The female can be distinguished by the brownish black primaries; the male's are black.

The Budgerigar: Undoubtedly the most popular of all the Grass Parrakeets is the Budgerigar *(Melopsittacus undulatus)*. Among domesticated birds, only the Canary has attained equal renown. The Budgerigar (often known as 'Parakeet' in the USA) is the beginner's bird *par excellence*. Hardy, prolific in cage or aviary and available in an immense range and combination of colours, it is the ideal subject for pet-keeper or breeder. A few pairs for breeding will provide experience of the breeding cycle and its problems and delights. The most common mistake of newcomers to parrot-breeding is an over-ambitious start with species which are expensive and not free-breeding. The heartache and failure which follows often induces the beginner to give up. Not only that, inexperienced keepers may inflict unconscious suffering on the larger parrots because they do not fully understand their requirements. The interest of the beginner who starts with Budgerigars is likely to be maintained and, in all likelihood, the progression to the more difficult species will be less fraught with difficulties.

Budgerigars will rear young in cages which should be in the region of 91 cm (3 ft) long, or in aviaries on the colony system. The latter method is favoured by beginners whose main aim is an aviary full of colourful birds. Serious breeders invariably choose the cage system because of the necessity of controlling pairings.

Two important factors should be borne in mind by the colony-breeder:

a) Initially, all the birds must be placed in the aviary at the same time. Birds added later are likely to be attacked.
b) Twice as many nest-boxes as there are pairs should be erected, to help prevent the squabbling which invariably arises in any colony. The individual responsible must be removed, along with his or her mate, if the harmony of the group is being disrupted.

Sexing adult Budgerigars of most colours is a simple matter. The cere, the area of bare skin above the beak, is blue in males and brown in females. In certain colours, including Lutinos and Albinos (red-eyed birds with pure yellow or pure white plumage) and some Pieds, the cere is pale mauve in males. In young Budgerigars, the cere is mauvish blue in males and whitish blue or white in females. This knowledge is essential when choosing a young bird as a pet, as the choice of most people will be a male. Generally they are more gentle and make more talented talkers.

6

OTHER AVIARY PARROTS

In Europe, Australian species make up a very large proportion of the parrots kept in aviaries – if we exclude one very important species, the Peach-faced Lovebird.

LOVEBIRDS

The immense popularity of the Lovebirds *(Agapornis* spp.*)* equals or surpasses that of the Grass Parrakeets *(Neophema* spp.*)*. Yet it is based on the one extremely prolific species. In a little more than a decade, the Peach-faced Lovebird *(A. roseicollis)* has produced more mutations than any species of parrot to date, other than the Budgerigar. A list issued by a top American breeder in 1984 included more than thirty mutations offered for sale. These included two types of Cinnamons in nine shades, Lutino, Albino, two mutations of Pied in eight colours, three shades of green, three shades of blue, a White, a Yellow, and a White-faced Blue. As with the Budgerigar, more than one mutation can be combined, offering an endless range of colours and mutations and limitless possibilities to those interested in genetics. It is no wonder that this free-breeding bird has acquired more new devotees during the past decade than probably any other Parrot.

Peach-faced Lovebird

The wild-type Peach-faced Lovebird is green, with salmon pink face and upper breast and bright blue rump and upper tail coverts. There is a band of black near the base of the tail and red patches at the base. Immature birds have softer colours; the face is pale pink; part of the upper mandible is blackish.

The size of this species, 15 cm (6 in) in length, is one reason for its popularity. Being small, it does not require spacious accommodation and, in fact, breeds just as freely in a cage as in an aviary. The breeding cage should be a wooden structure with a wire front, measuring not less than 91 cm (3 ft) long. Because this species builds a bulky nest, the nest-box should be larger than one offered to other birds of this size; suggested dimensions are 23 cm (9 in) long, 15 cm (6 in) wide and 17 cm (7 in) high with an entrance hole 7 cm (3 in) in diameter. As nesting material, Lovebirds can be offered branches of willow, from which they will strip the bark, also long grass, cuttings from honeysuckle and strips of newspaper.

The main problem in breeding this and most other Lovebirds is that of sexing them. In the commonly available species, the plumage of the male and female is alike. Because the value of the Normal and some of the more common mutations is not high, and surgical sexing (see p.74) may cost more than the bird is worth, most Lovebird-breeders do not have their birds sexed. Those who breed from the sex-

Figure 21. (Left) Peach-faced Lovebirds. (Right) Blue Peach-faced Lovebirds.

linked mutations usually realise that there is a fool-proof method of sexing their offspring in the nest. For example, when a sex-linked male (e.g. Lutino, Albino, Cinnamon) is paired to a normal green female, all the birds of the sex-linked colours, distinguished on hatching by their red eyes, will be females and all the Normals will be males.

The nest-box is best placed on the outside of the cage for ease of inspection. Few true pairs fail to make an attempt to nest so if no eggs are laid, the 'pair' probably consists of two males. An abnormally large clutch may indicate two females. The normal clutch size is about five. The eggs are incubated for about 23 days by the female only; the young spend 6 or 7 weeks in the nest. If they are to be sold as pets, they should be caged indoors for a few days to accustom them to the close proximity of people. In the UK, few Lovebirds are kept as pets; probably 95 per cent of those sold are bought for breeding purposes.

Their small size makes them good subjects for those without aviaries. A worthwhile number of breeding cages can be contained in a small indoor or outdoor birdroom. Better results will be gained using this method than the colony system, as Peach-faceds can be very aggressive during the breeding season. Fights will ensue, with the possible loss of eggs or young, if a hen enters another's nest-box. Lovebirds should not be kept with Finches or any birds smaller than themselves, as they can prove very vicious. Neither should they be kept with Budgerigars.

Another 'don't' where Lovebirds are concerned is the practice of hybridising two species. This is a waste of existing pure stock; some hybrids may bear a strong resemblance to one parent and, if used in the mistaken belief that they are pure-bred, or for any other reason, they spoil the quality and purity of existing stocks of Peach-faced Lovebirds. Hybrid Lovebirds, despite their attractive appearance, have a low monetary value, as no serious breeder would purchase such birds.

The Masked and Fischer's Lovebirds

Two other species of Lovebird can be considered free-breeding, the Masked *(A. personata)* and the Fischer's *(A. fischeri)*. The latter generally does quite well on the colony system, unlike the other Lovebirds, but it is advisable to remember that, for a harmonious group, all the members should be placed in the aviary at the same time after which no further additions should be made.

Figure 22. Fischer's Lovebirds.

CONURES

Another group which has much to recommend it are the Conures; unfortunately, most Conures also have one disadvantage – loud voices. If this is not an important consideration, these Neotropical parrakeets provide colour and character, the latter trait being one which is less obvious in the Lovebirds. Conures are cheeky, inquisitive and usually very intelligent. Many of those available are imported birds but the number being bred increases annually.

Points to bear in mind when housing Conures are that they can be destructive to woodwork, they have a talent for finding their way out of small holes (thus aviaries must be carefully maintained) and most require a nest-box for roosting in all the year round.

There are more than thirty species of Conure, the majority of which belong to

Figure 23. The Green-cheeked Conure *(Pyrrhura molinae)* is a prolific species.

Figure 24. The Golden-capped Conure *(Aratinga auricapilla)* is an example of a species whose habitat is being destroyed but which is breeding freely in captivity and being conserved by aviculturists.

two genera: *Aratinga* and *Pyrrhura*. The two groups differ in important respects: *Aratinga* Conures have much louder, harsher voices and their plumage is basically green, adorned with small areas of one colour, such as orange, red or blue on the head or under the wing. *Pyrrhura* Conures, on the other hand, have quieter voices, are less destructive and have more ornate colouration; typically the feathers of neck and breast are conspicuously margined with white or with a light colour. Many pairs are very prolific and habitually lay seven or eight eggs. *Pyrrhura* Conures are very highly recommended; the main drawback is that, with the exception of the Red-bellied *(P. frontalis)*, they are not readily available. However, they are worth making an effort to obtain.

In all Conures, the tail accounts for between one half and one third of the total length. The Red-bellied measures about 10 in (25 cm) overall. The conspicuous white eye ring contrasts with the dark green plumage, the maroon forehead, brownish ear coverts and the irregular patch of maroon on the abdomen. The feathers of the side of the neck and upper breast are broadly margined with yellow and yellowish white, to produce the markings typical of the genus, which are especially pronounced in this species. The upper surface of the tail is reddish, green at the base; the underside is maroon. Sexes are alike and young birds do not differ significantly from adults; indeed they are indistinguishable within a few weeks. Fitting split rings while the young are in the nest is therefore advisable if they are to be retained. The presence of the young usually deters the parents from nesting again, so they should be removed to another aviary when they are independent, or their parents should be provided with a second nest-box.

Aratinga Conures are imported more regularly and in larger numbers and consequently they are less expensive. The choice of species is wide. One of the few in which more aviary-bred than imported specimens are available is the Sun Conure *(A. solstitialis)*, one of the most beautiful parrots in aviculture and among the most expensive of the Conures. About the same size as the Red-bellied, also with a conspicuous white area of skin around the eye and a black beak, there the resemblance ends. The plumage is of varying shades of yellow and orange, fiery in areas, only part of the wings and tail being green. Young birds are much greener than adults.

Hand-reared youngsters make extremely desirable pets (except for their voices) and find a ready market at a price which is worthwhile to the breeder. An initial problem in breeding this species and, indeed, all Conures, is identifying the sexes. Male and female are alike in appearance and behaviour is not any indication of sex, since a close bond may exist between two males or two females, which behave exactly as one would expect of a true pair, except for the production of fertile eggs. Surgical sexing is recommended from the outset.

Approximately 24 days is the length of the incubation period in Conures; only the female incubates. Young remain in the nest for between 7½ and 8 weeks. Although the nest-box should be left in position all the year, they seldom attempt to breed during the winter, unlike Peach-faced Lovebirds, for example, who often fledge chicks during the coldest months of the year.

The recommended size for an enclosure for a pair of Red-bellied or Sun Conures is 240 cm (8 ft) long, 91 cm (3 ft) wide and 180 cm (6 ft) high. A longer flight will be fully utilised.

KAKARIKIS

The parrakeets from New Zealand, known to aviculturists as Kakarikis, are equally as active and inquisitive as the Conures. Their mannerisms are quite different; they have long legs, move around jerkily, like to scratch on the ground and can run up and down wire netting. They are extremely attractive aviary birds and they are exceptionally prolific. Unfortunately, they are not renowned for longevity, but careful management can help them to reach their potential lifespan (12-year-old pairs have been reported). The following points should be noted to this end:

a) They need to be wormed regularly.
b) Females younger than 6 months of age should not be allowed to breed. Nest-boxes should be removed in the winter. Both measures are designed to reduce the incidence of egg-binding.
c) The diet should be varied; the proportion of dry seed should be no higher than 60 per cent.

Figure 25. Yellow-fronted Kakarikis a few days after fledging.

Kakarikis can be recommended for their friendly personalities and for their readiness to breed. They commence to nest at a very early age, if given the opportunity: between 4 and 5 months. The clutch numbers from five to nine eggs; these are incubated by the female for 21 days. Chicks spend 5 to 6 weeks in the nest-box. The latter should be large as Kakarikis are susceptible to heat stress; the suggested size is 31 cm (12 in) × 23 cm (9 in) × 25 cm (10 in) high. The feeding of the first-round young after they leave the nest is usually left to the male because the female is incubating another clutch of eggs. The male's behaviour should be closely observed because some will kill their male offspring.

The aviary for a pair of Kakarikis should measure approximately 300 cm (10 ft) long, 100 cm (3¼ ft) wide and 180 cm (6 ft) high. It should have a shelter into which the birds can be shut in inclement weather.

Particular attention should be given to providing a varied and nutritious diet. Sunflower seed should be given soaked or sprouted, rather than dry, except in very warm climates. Dry Canary seed and white millet should also be provided. An abundance of fresh green foods is essential, especially when the birds are rearing young. At that time a more substantial rearing food, such as Canary eggfood or bread and milk, must also be provided, especially to pairs with more than three or four chicks. Five to eight eggs is the normal clutch. Fruit and the berries of such shrubs as *Cotoneaster, Pyracantha* and elder, will be relished. Sweetcorn and corn on the cob can also be provided. It is well worth expending a little extra effort to produce nests of healthy young; a mainly seed diet will not keep these birds in good health over a long period.

Red-fronted Kakarikis *(Cyanoramphus novaezelandiae)* measure about 28 cm (11 in) long, the females being slightly smaller. The Yellow-fronted *(C. auriceps)* is a little smaller. Both are mainly green; the Red-fronted has the forehead and a patch behind the eye red, while the Yellow-fronted has a narrow red line above the forehead followed by a substantial area of yellow, and no red patch behind the eye. The two species will hybridise readily if allowed to do so, but hybridising must be discouraged.

ASIATIC PARRAKEETS

The parrakeets of Asia are classified in the genus *Psittacula*. It should be noted that in all these parrakeets, the female is the dominant member of a pair. The male requires a protracted ritualised courtship to overcome his fear of his mate. For this reason, male and female should be introduced several months before the start of the breeding season.

Ringneck Parrakeets

By far the best known and the most prolific is the Indian Ringneck Parrakeet *(P. krameri manillensis)*. The African Ringneck *(P.k. krameri)* is less well known. It is smaller with a less heavy beak, darker red upper mandible, tending to blackish, and brighter head colouration. The Indian species is a pleasing soft shade of green,

Figure 26. (Left) Normal Ringneck Parrakeet. (Right) Lutino Ringneck Parrakeet.

brightest on the cheeks. The male only has a black ring encircling the neck, edged with pink at the back of the neck. The upper mandible is dark red and the lower mandible black. The central feathers of the very long tail are bluish. Total length is about 40 cm (15 in). The body size is relatively small; this species weighs about 115 g (4 oz) or twice as much as a Peach-faced Lovebird, for example.

It should be noted that females and immature birds lack the head markings. Males acquire the neck ring at the third moult, i.e, at 2½ years old. In most parrots, males outnumber females, but this seems very noticeable with *Psittacula* parrakeets, of which there is always a shortage of females.

As aviary birds, Ringnecks have a number of advantages. They are very hardy, long-lived, free-breeding and, when adult, sexed at a glance. Inexpensive and readily obtainable, they are birds of graceful proportions which look well in an aviary. Unsuited to the confines of cage life, they should not be considered when choosing a pet.

Several mutations are available, the best known of which are the Lutino and the Blue. Albinos, Cinnamons, Greys and Pieds are bred in much smaller numbers, but the potential for a wide range of mutations exists.

Two points should be borne in mind when keeping *Psittacula* parrakeets. They are highly susceptible to frostbite, which can result in the loss of toes (not just nails). They should therefore be encouraged to roost in an enclosed shelter during the colder months. However, they are earlier nesters than any other species described within these pages; February is the usual laying month. It is a mistake to withhold nest-boxes in the hope that they will nest later in the year. If the normal breeding cycle is interfered with, they may not lay at all. For this reason the nest-box should be in position by the beginning of February. It should measure approximately 25 cm (10 in) square and 76 cm (30 in) high. Three to five eggs are laid and incubated by the female for a minimum of 23 days. Young birds leave the nest at about 50 days old. It is unusual for Ringnecks to be double-brooded if the breeding cycle reaches the chick stage.

Alexandrine Parrakeet

The Alexandrine Parrakeet *(P. eupatria)* is a larger version of the Ringneck, differing in that the male has dark red shoulder patches. The body weight is double that of the Ringneck. The Alexandrine is a very destructive bird with a large, powerful beak. Highly intelligent, it is a rewarding species to keep and worth the effort of constructing a metal-framed aviary.

The Alexandrine lays two or three eggs which are incubated for about 28 days. Young leave the nest after 7 weeks. The very attractive Lutino mutation is the only one which is firmly established.

Figure 27. Male Alexandrine Parrakeet – intelligent and attractive but destructive in an aviary.

Plumhead Parrakeet

In complete contrast to the Alexandrine is one of the smallest and arguably the most beautiful member of the genus, the Plumhead Parrakeet *(P. cyanocephala)*. Gentle and quiet, it is suitable for those whose neighbours would object to the strident tones of the Ringneck and Alexandrine. Weighing only about 70 g (2 ½ oz)

Figure 28. The very beautiful Plumhead Parrakeet *(Psittacula cyanocephala)*.

yet measuring about 33 cm (13 in), it too has a very long tail – dark blue, tipped with white. The male is exquisitely and unusually coloured: the head is plum-coloured with a bluish purple cast; black moustache markings diminish into a narrow collar. There is a maroon patch on the wing and the rest of the plumage is varying shades of green. The female has a bluish grey head with a dull yellow collar; she lacks the maroon wing patch of the male. Immature birds are all green, with the head greyish green; at the first moult, the males resemble the females. Males can usually be distinguished at an early age when they start to display – jumping on the perch, swirling the head and warbling.

In this species the usual clutch is four eggs and these are incubated for a minimum of 22 days by the female. The young leave the nest after 7 weeks.

LORIES AND LORIKEETS

Few parrots are more colourful in personality and plumage than the Lories. These are the Brush-tongued Parrots, whose diet consists largely of pollen and nectar. In captivity, they readily accept a liquid food made up from such items as malt extract, glucose or honey, baby cereals, invalid foods such as Complan, and condensed milk. Because of the liquid nature of the droppings, outdoor aviaries are the only practical form of accommodation.

In addition to the nectar mixture, some Lories will eat seed, but this should be limited, and sunflower is best offered soaked, not dry. The usual fruits and green foods should also be available and, for those birds who refuse them, they should be liquidised and added to the nectar mixture.

The liquid food for Lories must be offered fresh at least once daily, and twice or even more in extreme weather conditions. The pleasure of their company is, however, well worth the extra attention involved.

The charm of Lories in aviaries is that they are exceptionally entertaining and playful. Most become tame. They are avid bathers and should have a large container for this purpose which is refilled daily.

When buying Lories, their mouths should be inspected. They are very susceptible to the fungus, *Candida albicans*, which can grow anywhere inside the mouth, including under the tongue. It is whitish in appearance and causes lesions which can bleed if removal is attempted. The correct treatment is application at least twice daily of Fungillin® suspension; a prescription for this can be obtained from a veterinarian. The fungus may grow as a result of the birds being kept in unhygienic conditions, or may be due to stress or a dietary deficiency, especially lack of Vitamin A and an excess of sugar in the diet.

The normal clutch size in all but the Australian Lories (and the Perfect Lorikeet which lays three eggs) is two. The incubation period is 23 or 24 days and the young remain in the nest for from 8 weeks (Goldie's) to 10 weeks (Dusky Lories). Only the female incubates but both sexes tend the young.

The Lories originate from Australia, New Guinea and Indonesia. Two of the most popular and free-breeding, Goldie's Lorikeet and the Dusky Lory, are from New Guinea.

Goldie's Lorikeet

Perhaps destined to be the first completely domesticated Lory is Goldie's Lorikeet *(Trichoglossus goldiei)*. Only 19 cm (7 in) in length, it has proved a ready breeder in cages of the type used for breeding Budgerigars, i.e. about 91 cm (3 ft) long. Some pairs will accept a Budgerigar nest-box, or one measuring about 15 cm (6 in) square and 25 cm (10 in) high. Nesting material should consist of peat or compressed wood shavings (pet litter) obtainable from some pet-shops. Drainage holes should be drilled in the bottom. It is normal for Lories to roost in their nest-boxes, which must therefore be left in position throughout the year.

Goldie's Lorikeet has every advantage except that of being readily sexable. It is pretty, quiet, not destructive and very willing to breed. Recognised by the red forehead and black beak, the crown and eyes are bordered with mauve and the cheeks and ear coverts are bluish pink. The plumage is dark green above and light green streaked with darker green below. Immature birds are much duller counterparts of the adults.

Figure 29. Goldie's Lorikeets (shortly before leaving the nest) aged 8½ weeks.

Figure 30. Red or Moluccan Lory.

Dusky Lory

The Dusky Lory *(Pseudeos fuscata)* is equally free-breeding. A considerably larger bird, it measures about 25 cm (10 in) in length. Plumage is variable, there being an orange phase and a yellow phase. It can be described briefly as being dark brown above and brown marked with orange or yellow patches and bands below. However, many other colours in the plumage are revealed on close inspection. The iris of the eye and the beak are orange in adults, brownish in young birds.

7

THE IMPORTANCE OF CORRECT FEEDING

For all but the more highly domesticated of captive parrots, feeding is undoubtedly the most important aspect of their care. It is no accident that the species which could be considered totally domesticated are those which require the least demanding diets. Among exotic birds as a whole, it is the softbills which are least bred and rarely reared to more than one generation. This is mainly because their food is more difficult and expensive to acquire and therefore relatively few people are prepared to go to the trouble and expense entailed.

The parrot species which are most popular with bird-keepers – Cockatiels, Budgerigars and other Australian parrakeets – are birds which exist largely on seeds in the wild. Seed is the easiest form of nutrient to provide for captive birds. Unfortunately, as a result, it has been assumed over the years that most parrots are seedeaters. While it is true that most will eat seed, by far the majority of parrots are not granivorous but omnivorous. There are many, even the majority, which could spend long and healthy lives without ever seeing a seed.

'Omnivorous' is the term used for animals which feed on a wide variety of foods. Typical omnivorous British species are Jays, Jackdaws and Gulls. They feed on animal and vegetable foods – and so do most parrots if they have the chance, in the wild and in captivity. Many species take insects and some eat carrion – dead animals and birds. It seems very likely that small living animals, such as lizards, are eaten by some parrots on occasions. Buds, fruits and leaves, also seeds, form the main part of the diet of most parrots, however. They will also take nectar from flowers, or even eat the flowers themselves.

Dry seed is therefore a poor substitute for the varied diet which a wild parrot enjoys. Not only is it deficient in certain respects but, in large quantities, some seeds, such as sunflower and hemp, cause diseases of the liver and other organs, because of their high oil content.

The assumption, which has grown up over the years, that the larger parrots should exist mainly on sunflower seed is gradually being dispelled, but this will be a slow process. A letter which I received precisely as I started this chapter illustrates the point very well indeed. It was from a lady who had bought a young Blue-fronted Amazon 6 weeks previously. She was worried about its diet, which consisted of peanuts, spray millet (other seeds were refused), tangerines, apples, digestive biscuit, dog's marrow-bone biscuit and, once a week, well cooked lamb bones. She had written to the secretary of a parrot society who suggested buying another bird to teach it to eat 'normal' food. My reply was to the effect that her Amazon's diet was excellent – varied and nutritious. From the peanuts, lamb bones and spray millet, the bird would get protein (peanuts are high in this – about 28 per cent), from the tangerines, Vitamin C and from the peanuts, Vitamin B.

The Amazon was also receiving a vitamin/mineral supplement (SA 37®) on its food. It therefore seems unlikely that its diet was deficient in any respect or that it was receiving an excess of anything. Peanuts are quite safe to feed to birds, in the shell or shelled, provided that high-grade peanuts meant for human consumption are offered. (Peanuts may harbour a mould which is highly toxic.)

The diet described above for the Amazon is, in my opinion, superior to that offered to most pet parrots, i.e. proprietary parrot food, which consists largely of sunflower seed, together with a small amount of fruits and vegetables. In other words, it does not matter if a parrot refuses what is considered a more orthodox diet as long as it is receiving the nutrients it requires – protein, some carbohydrate, vitamins and fibre (the latter for the efficient functioning of the digestive system).

During the war years, when seed was virtually unobtainable, most parrots existed on table scraps. There is absolutely nothing wrong with this provided that a little common sense is exercised in the foods given and their quantity. Greasy foods and rich foods should, of course, be avoided, but most of the more usual food items (not including 'junk' foods) are excellent for parrots – cheese, meat, bread, toast, hard-boiled egg, biscuits and fruit and vegetables (cooked and uncooked). Apparently, an exception is avocado pear.

No problems should be experienced in feeding domesticated species, such as Australian parrakeets, Cockatiels and Lovebirds. Seed will form by far the largest proportion of their diet, plus green food and vegetables to a lesser or greater degree. When they are feeding young, a rearing food, such as bread and milk or a proprietary Canary-rearing food, will be required.

However, in the case of non-domesticated species – and especially wild-caught birds – the requirements are not quite so easily fulfilled. It is advisable to learn about the natural diet of the species in question. Much valuable information on this aspect can be gained from Joseph Forshaw's *Parrots of the World*. (Copies can be obtained through specialist booksellers and libraries with ease.) Perhaps only a few lines of information are available, but they should be sufficient to form a basis for a diet.

The problem is often that, from the time the birds have been in captivity, sunflower seed has figured largely in the diet and, initially, all other items are refused. This is common but, with perseverance, it can be rectified. The first step is to soak the sunflower seed in water for 24 hours, rinse it well under a running tap and then supply it in a container on its own, so that its dampness does not affect other foods. Soaked rather than dry sunflower is preferred by most parrots. The next step is to offer sunflower seed in a sprouted state. After it has been soaked, it should be left in a warm place until the shoots are about 6 mm (¼ in) long. They may taste bitter when they exceed about 13 mm (½ in) in length. The food value of sprouted seeds increases substantially, especially the vitamin content. They are also more easily digested and therefore more suitable for birds which are feeding young.

Also suitable for sprouting are mung beans, which can be obtained from health food stores and supermarkets. These small green beans are best sprouted with the aid of a salad-sprouter. One with three sections is useful as, unless the weather is

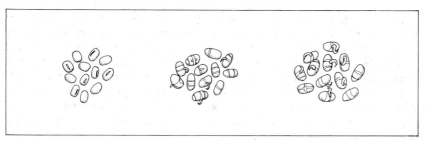

Figure 31. Mung beans: (left) before sprouting; (centre) commencing to sprout; (right) more advanced stage of germination.

Figure 32. Mung beans can be sprouted in a salad sprouter. Pour water over them daily and in about 3 days they will be ready for feeding to your birds.

warm, the beans take about 3 days to sprout, thus the contents of a layer of the sprouter can be used daily and re-filled. Simply run water through the sprouter once daily, then wash the beans in running water before use and allow excess moisture to drain off. All bean sprouts are rich in vitamins of the B complex and contain a higher level of protein and amino acids than most vegetables.

I have tried other beans, including soya beans, but most parrots waste these. They should be persevered with because their protein content is very high (higher than meat, eggs or cheese, and double that of cereals), yet they are low in carbohydrates and fat. Even a few eaten daily are valuable. Mung beans are much more acceptable. An appetising mixture can be made up using fresh or frozen peas, sweetcorn and mung beans.

Sweetcorn is, of course, an extremely valuable food for parrots. Most find fresh corn on the cob irresistible. Frozen sweetcorn which has been thawed is usually equally acceptable. It is an excellent food for breeding birds, before the breeding season as a conditioner, and especially while young are being reared, being readily accepted by most parrots, from the smallest Lories to the largest Macaws. Those with large-capacity freezers would be advised to buy corn cobs in quantity in the autumn when their price is low, blanch them and freeze them for future use. Cobs can be chopped into sections about 2.5 cm (1 in) long to avoid wastage. In the USA, where corn cobs are very much less expensive than in the UK, they are used far more extensively. A favourite with Cockatoos, they can be the means of persuading conservative feeders to sample something other than seed.

Parrots are wasteful feeders, often taking only a bite or two from an item of food before discarding it in favour of another – just as they do in the wild. Chopping fruit and vegetables into small pieces therefore helps to prevent wastage.

Two vegetables which I use extensively are carrot (which contains Vitamin A) and celery. They can be cut into small pieces for small species; larger birds prefer longer pieces which they can hold in the foot and nibble at. Both should be washed well before being fed in a raw state. The green, crisp, Israeli celery is a great favourite with many parrots. The leafy parts can be fed as a substitute for green food when it is in short supply. The firmer parts are relished by most large parrots, including hard-to-please Cockatoos; celery is especially valuable for Eclectus Parrots which have a great need for fibre in their diet.

Most green foods consist largely of water, but this fact should not lead to them being undervalued. Apart from the essential vitamin content (parrots require Vitamins A and B and appear to have little need for Vitamin C), these foods are enjoyed for their texture, for the pleasure gained from shredding them and for the variety which they add to the diet. Lettuce, for example, is low in food value but high in amusement value. Very high in food value is lucerne (alfalfa). It contains up to 19 per cent protein, is rich in calcium, iron and various minerals and vitamins.

Other suitable green foods are spinach (the perpetual kind can be grown year round) and watercress; both contain Vitamin A and watercress is noted for its iron content. Wild foods, such as chickweed, seeding grasses, sowthistle, young dandelion leaves and coltsfoot, can be offered, provided that they are gathered in an area uncontaminated by pesticides.

Among the most valuable of wild foods are berries. Few parrots can resist those of hawthorn and elderberries are popular with many species. Great enjoyment is gained from nibbling the twigs of hawthorn.

The variety of fruits which can be offered is also wide. Of the seasonal fruits, pomegranates and cherries are probably the most highly favoured; strawberries, peaches and plums are not generally liked. Of those available all year round, apple, pear, grapes and orange are most readily accepted. Some parrots will remove the pips from the grapes (or the stone from the cherry) and discard the rest. Much fruit will be wasted unless it is cut into small pieces. The quantity of fruit taken will depend to a great degree on the species; Australian parrakeets take little but Neotropical species (especially Conures and Caiques) consume very much larger amounts. It should be remembered that fruit, with its moist surface, is a good receptacle for antibiotics and other medicine, when the need arises. It can also be a means of taming birds, as many parrots will take fruit – and not other foods – from the hand.

Never lose sight of the fact that parrots, especially the larger species, really enjoy their food. This is one reason why pellets formulated for feeding parrots were not successful; parrots simply will not eat dry, pelleted foods. Many birds have little sense of taste, but this is not true of parrots. They are believed to have more taste-buds than most birds. Whether or not this is so, they are far more discerning in their preferences and many have pronounced likes and dislikes, favouring some items to the degree that they renounce their usual caution in an effort to reach them. Cheese, toast, millet spray, corn, cherries and hawthorn berries are among the items which most often meet with passionate approval. While they tend to be the more expensive foods, few are as expensive as sunflower seed!

Parrots which receive a varied diet are happier, healthier and less likely to suffer from boredom. Where large parrots are concerned, some consideration should be given to providing small seeds, such as spray millet and white millet, whose consumption will keep them occupied for long periods, rather than gaining all their nourishment in a few minutes from, for example, sunflower seed.

No matter how varied the diet offered, it is of little use unless the birds actually eat the items offered, rather than confining their attentions to two or three favourite items. Some birds favour a very restricted diet and these should be encouraged to widen their tastes by withholding the favourite items until late in the day, or housing them with or near birds which are less conservative. Less favoured items should be persevered with up to a point – after which one is merely wasting time and money. It is necessary to know every bird as an individual in order to prevent waste and present them with foods they will eat.

It must also be remembered that birds kept on the colony system may be dominated by those highest in the pecking order, who may regularly take all the choice items. If this occurs, a number of feeding points must be provided. It may even be necessary to provide two feeding points in an aviary inhabited by only one pair, e.g. if one bird is dominant or the two birds have recently been introduced and one is lacking in confidence.

Purchase and storage of seed and other foods is deserving of careful thought.

Except when a small number of birds is kept, it is advisable to buy seed in bulk from a reputable seed merchant. Send for samples from several and compare them for cleanliness and quality. Sunflower, for example, should possess plump kernels, not thin ones. Samples of pine nuts, beloved by the larger parrots, should be broken open to ensure that a large number are not mouldy or rancid. Canary seed should be shiny, without many broken and husk-less seeds. A germination test can be carried out. How many seeds will sprout? The answer should be 'Nearly all of them'. If the proportion is low, it may mean that the seed has been in storage for a long period. This is seldom the case when buying from an importer or large seed merchant but far more likely when buying from a pet-shop, which may not have a large turnover of seed.

Do not buy more than about 3 months' supply of seed at one time. Store it in

Table 1. Recommended food items for various parrot groups

	sunflower	Canary seed	hemp	white millet	spray millet	peanuts	pine nuts	mung beans (sprouted)	apple	grapes	orange	celery	carrot	seedling grasses	chickweed	spinach	hawthorn berries	elderberries	bread and milk	cheese	sweet corn or corn on cob	nectar
Alexandrine Parrakeet	✓	✓	✓	✓	✓	✓	✓	✓	✓	✓	✓	✓	✓	✓	✓	✓	✓	✓	✓	✓	✓	–
Amazon Parrots	✓	✓	✓	✓	✓	✓	✓	✓	✓	✓	✓	✓	✓	★	✓	✓	✓	✓	✓	✓	✓	–
Large Macaws	✓	✓	✓	★	✓	✓	✓	✓	✓	✓	✓	✓	✓	✓	✓	✓	✓	✓	✓	✓	✓	–
Bourke's Parrakeet	✓	✓	✓	✓	✓	–	–	✓	✓	–	★	✓	✓	✓	✓	✓	★	✓	✓	–	✓	–
Budgerigar	–	✓	✓	✓	✓	–	–	✓	✓	–	★	★	✓	✓	✓	✓	–	✓	✓	–	✓	–
Cockatiel	★	✓	✓	✓	✓	–	–	★	★	–	–	★	★	✓	✓	✓	–	–	✓	–	✓	–
Cockatoos	✓	✓	✓	★	✓	✓	✓	✓	✓	✓	✓	✓	✓	✓	✓	✓	✓	✓	✓	✓	✓	–
Conures	✓	✓	✓	✓	✓	✓	★	✓	✓	✓	✓	✓	✓	✓	✓	✓	✓	✓	✓	✓	✓	–
Dusky Lory	★	–	–	–	✓	–	–	–	✓	✓	✓	–	–	✓	✓	✓	–	–	★	–	✓	✓
Golden-mantled Rosella	✓	✓	✓	✓	✓	✓	✓	✓	✓	✓	✓	✓	✓	✓	✓	✓	✓	✓	✓	✓	✓	–
Grey Parrot	✓	✓	✓	★	✓	✓	★	✓	✓	✓	✓	✓	★	★	✓	✓	✓	✓	★	✓	✓	–
Kakarikis	✓	✓	✓	✓	✓	✓	–	✓	✓	✓	✓	✓	✓	✓	✓	✓	✓	✓	✓	✓	✓	–
Peach-faced Lovebird	✓	✓	✓	✓	✓	–	–	✓	✓	✓	✓	★	★	✓	✓	✓	–	–	✓	–	✓	–
Plumhead & Ringneck Parrakeets	✓	✓	✓	✓	✓	★	–	✓	✓	✓	✓	–	✓	✓	✓	✓	★	✓	✓	–	✓	–
Redrump Parrakeet	✓	✓	✓	✓	✓	✓	–	✓	✓	✓	✓	★	✓	✓	✓	✓	✓	✓	✓	–	✓	–
Senegal Parrot	✓	✓	✓	✓	✓	✓	✓	✓	✓	✓	✓	✓	✓	✓	✓	✓	✓	✓	✓	✓	✓	–
Small Macaws	✓	✓	✓	✓	✓	✓	✓	✓	✓	✓	✓	✓	✓	✓	✓	✓	✓	✓	✓	✓	✓	–
Splendid Parrakeet	✓	✓	✓	✓	✓	–	–	✓	✓	–	–	–	★	✓	✓	✓	–	★	✓	–	✓	–
Stanley Rosella	✓	✓	✓	✓	✓	✓	–	✓	✓	✓	✓	✓	✓	✓	✓	✓	✓	✓	✓	–	✓	–
Turquoisine Parrakeet	✓	✓	✓	✓	✓	–	–	✓	✓	–	–	–	★	✓	✓	✓	–	★	✓	–	✓	–

★ Some birds may not take this item

70

plastic dustbins or other vermin-proof containers. The storage area must be dry and clean. Mouldy seed can be lethal.

Buy good-quality fruit and vegetables. The larger parrots are very discerning and can distinguish, for example, different varieties of apples. Give all birds who will take them occasional or regular treats of such items as cheese, wheat or bran biscuits, meat bones and millet spray. This includes aviary birds: they look forward to such tit-bits which must add enjoyment to their routine existence.

Do not discard any nutritious food from the kitchen without considering whether it would be eaten by any aviary or pet parrots. Bread, for example, need never be wasted. It can be offered in the form of bread and milk or stale bread can be baked in the oven then cut into crunchy squares.

Aim to persuade your birds to consume a wide variety of foods; dependence on one item is especially inadvisable when that item is sunflower seed. The day may come when so much sunflower seed is processed for human use that only small amounts are available – at very high prices – to seed merchants. Table 1 (left) provides examples of what can be offered to various groups of parrots. Many other items could have been included.

It must be remembered that a bird's dietary requirements are not the same throughout the year. For example, when breeding and when moulting, it has a greater need for protein. Some foods may not be suitable at all times; seeds which are high in oil, such as hemp and sunflower, should be fed more sparingly in warm weather. Other foods should be fed with care at certain times. For example, sunflower seed should be fed soaked (see p.66) not dry, to birds with young. It is easier to digest. Some birds feed whole sunflower seeds to young chicks, causing compaction of the crop. This is less likely to occur if the seed has been soaked prior to feeding.

Figure 33. This range of seeds and nuts can be used to make up a parrot mixture or fed individually.

Parrakeets and other species need an abundance of fresh green foods when rearing young and providing this several times daily stimulates them to feed their chicks. Bread and milk or a proprietary Canary-rearing food is excellent for birds which are feeding chicks but not usually necessary at other times of the year, except as an occasional treat.

Finally, remember that variety is not only the spice of life but it can be the giver of life. Breeding birds offered a limited diet may be lacking in some essential nutrient without which they are unable to breed.

8

BREEDING

The enormous pleasure to be derived from breeding birds, rather than merely keeping them, has to be experienced to be believed. To those who are deeply absorbed in birds, it provides a satisfaction found in few other areas of life.

I will repeat my earlier advice not to start too ambitiously. Species which nest readily, such as Budgerigars, Cockatiels and Lovebirds, are the most suitable for the beginner. They provide encouragement and experience. The birds themselves are relatively inexpensive and their cost is likely to be recouped by the sale of young. Those who start off with large expensive parrots will have either years of frustration ahead (unless they are inordinately lucky) or they will soon suffer disillusionment and turn to another hobby.

Suitable species with which to make a start, and information concerning their breeding habits, is given in Chapters 5 and 6. In this chapter, I will outline some of the problems and pitfalls likely to be encountered. For more extensive information on the subject, the reader is referred to *Parrots, Their Care and Breeding*.

COMMON ERRORS

A common mistake of the beginner is to attempt to keep several breeding pairs in the same aviary. This usually leads to fighting, especially when several species are housed together. Generally, only Cockatiels nest satisfactorily on the colony system. If breeding is the aim, the rule should be one pair per aviary.

Another common error is obtaining birds unsuitable for breeding. An attempt should be made to make up young, unrelated pairs, by purchasing from two breeders or from one breeder who has two or more unrelated pairs of the species in question. Young birds should be obtained to ensure that they are not birds which have proved unsuitable for breeding, and unrelated birds are more likely to produce healthy young (provided that they are correctly cared for) than those which are closely related.

PAIRING

Perhaps the two most important factors in breeding parrots are compatibility of male and female, and varied and nutritious food. Without the first, no young will be produced, and without the second the young will succumb or will be of inferior quality. Never underestimate the importance of compatibility, especially with the larger parrots. Some pairs are instantly compatible, others take many months to settle down together and, rarely, some never do so.

In species which are not sexually dimorphic, (i.e. where the plumage and

73

outward appearance is the same in male and female), do not rely on behaviour as an indication of sex. The number of veterinarians practising surgical sexing is gradually increasing. This is something which commenced in the UK in the late 1970s and early 1980s (earlier in the USA) so do not necessarily expect to find a veterinarian in your area who can carry this out, but make enquiries at an area branch of the Parrot Society. Surgical sexing is carred out at some meetings by a qualified veterinarian. A small incision is made in the side of the bird (after administering an anaesthetic) and an endoscope is inserted through which the ovaries or testicles can be viewed. In addition to indicating the sex, it is possible to ascertain whether the bird is in breeding condition, or past reproductive age; it can also be used to discover whether any of the major organs display abnormalities. Thus surgical sexing can prevent years of attempting to breed with a totally unsuitable bird.

NESTING FACILITIES

Having obtained a true – and hopefully compatible – pair, and installed them in their breeding quarters, a nesting site must be provided. A wooden nest-box is best for most species. Suggested sizes are given in earlier chapters where various species are described and also in Table 2. Most beginners make the mistake of providing boxes which are too large for the species concerned, and with entrance holes which are far too big.

Table 2. Recommended sizes for nest-boxes

Species	Base	Height
Grass Parrakeets *(Neophema)*	20 × 20 cm (8 × 8 in)	31 cm (12 in)
Rosellas *(Platycercus)*	23 × 23 cm (9 × 9 in)	61-120 cm (24-48 in)
Kakarikis *(Cyanoramphus)*	23 × 23 cm (9 × 9 in)	31 cm (12 in)
Ringneck Parrakeets *(Psittacula)*	25 × 25 cm (10 × 10 in)	60 cm (24 in)
Hanging Parrots *(Loriculus)*	13 × 13 cm (5 × 5 in)	25 cm (10 in)
Lovebirds, Peach-faced, Fischer's and Masked *(Agapornis)*	23 × 15 cm (9 × 6 in)	17 cm (7 in)
Grey Parrot *(Psittacus)*	23 × 25 cm (9 × 10 in)	61 cm (24 in)
Amazon Parrots *(Amazona)*	23 × 25 cm (9 × 10 in)	61 cm (24 in)
Cockatiel *(Nymphicus)*	18 × 18 cm (7 × 7 in)	31 cm (12 in)
Conures *(Aratinga* and *Pyrrhura)*	18 × 18 cm (7 × 7 in)	25 cm (10 in)
Parrotlets *(Forpus)*	13 × 13 cm (5 × 5 in) (or a Budgerigar nest-box)	18 cm (7 in)
Dusky Lory *(Pseudeos)*	20 × 20 cm (8 × 8 in)	61 cm (24 in)
Goldie's Lorikeet *(Trichoglossus)*	13 × 13 cm (5 × 5 in)	23 cm (9 in)

All nest-boxes should have an inspection door in the side near the base – not in the top. This has two advantages: removal of eggs or chicks, should this be

Figure 34. The inspection door should be situated in the side of the nest-box not the top.

necessary, is facilitated; some females will panic if inspection is carried out from above as the only means of escape is towards the hand which has alarmed them.

Most parrots do not build a nest. The exceptions are Peach-faced and other Lovebirds which should be provided with willow twigs, and Quaker Parrakeets *(Myiopsitta monachus)* which build a bulky twig nest. In captivity, they will also use a nest-box. The only nesting material required for most birds is moss peat or pet-litter (obtained in compressed packs), or a mixture of the two.

Nest-boxes should face away from direct sunlight, or the interior of the box will be too light and too hot. The best position is the open flight, fitted securely high up, preferably with some means of protection from the elements on the roof over the nest. It is vitally important that they are waterproof. Stout timber is recommended, such as 19 mm (¾ in) plywood. Thick wood helps to retain warmth in the nest and makes it more difficult for the female to gnaw her way out or reduce the nest to the point of collapse. It helps to nail large pieces of wood inside which the female can gnaw while she is incubating.

EGGS

Egg-laying

A stage of the breeding cycle during which problems are often encountered is egg-laying. Most of them stem from a calcium deficiency. A large amount of calcium is required for egg-production; a deficiency results in soft-shelled eggs which the female finds difficult or impossible to expel, resulting in much pain in the first case and death in the second. Cuttlefish bone is the most usual source of calcium; milk (offer bread and milk) and cheese are other excellent sources. However, unless the diet also contains Vitamin D or unless the bird is exposed to sunlight, it will be unable to absorb the calcium. This is easily rectified by obtaining the liquid supplement (calcium and Vitamin D) Collo-Cal D® from a veterinarian. It has a strong taste but most birds will eat bread and milk or some other favourite item of food to which it has been added. It should also be added to the food of pairs rearing young indoors, or those which refuse items containing calcium, in order to prevent rickets in the young. Rickets is a common and tragic deformity of young birds, often manifesting itself in the form of splayed legs and soft, easily broken bones.

Egg-binding

This is the most common problem associated with laying. Egg-bound females normally leave the nest-box; a female in the early stages of incubation which leaves the nest and is seen sitting dejectedly on the perch, perhaps with wings drooping and eyes closed with pain, can be suspected of being egg-bound. Immediate action must be taken. The bird must be transferred very carefully to a small cage or hospital cage in a temperature of about 90° F (32° C). An infra-red lamp is an excellent source of heat for an egg-bound female. Normally, the heat will relax the

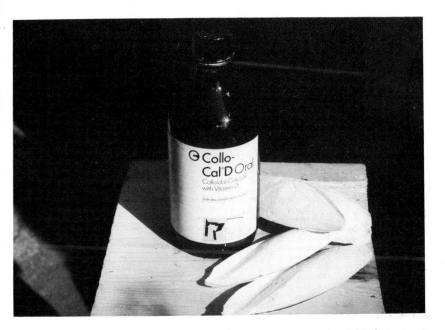

Figure 35. Calcium is vitally important in egg formation and, in chicks, for bone formation. Two good sources are a liquid calcium supplement and cuttlefish bone.

bird sufficiently for the egg to be laid. This will not necessarily occur that day; it is quite common for the egg not to be passed until the following day. If the bird appears very weak she may have been discovered too late and possibly be beyond help. But those discovered in good time usually lay without help (indeed, it is a mistake to interfere with the bird in any way), even if the egg is soft-shelled.

Collo-Cal D® should be added to the food and/or drinking water of an egg-bound hen so that the problem does not recur in subsequent eggs in the clutch. As a safety precaution, the bird should be retained indoors until the full clutch has been laid. Her eggs should be either fostered out or placed in an incubator. She probably will not be broody after being removed from her nest-box.

Egg-binding is most common during cold weather, which is why it is generally recommended that nest-boxes for most species should not be placed in position until the end of March or the beginning or middle of April, according to the weather.

Inspection of Nest

It is advisable to accustom most parrots and parrakeets to nest inspection prior to and during the incubation period. Unlike finches, for example, nest inspection does

Table 3. Guide to the lengths of incubation and fledging periods

Species	Incubation period in days	Approximate length of time young spend in nest
Cockatiel	19	4-5 weeks
Grass Parrakeets *(Neophema)*	18 or 19	28-30 days
Other Australian Parrakeets	19	5-6 weeks
Psittacula Parrakeets (Ringnecks, Plumheads etc)	24-28 (Longer in larger species)	7 weeks
Lovebirds	23	6-7 weeks
Kakarikis (New Zealand Parrakeets)	19	6-7 weeks
Hanging Parrots *(Loriculus)*	20	5 weeks
Cockatoos (white species)	28-30	9-12 weeks (Longer in larger species)
Roseate	25	6-7 weeks
Macaws { large species	28	Average 12 weeks
Macaws { small species	25-26	8-9 weeks
Conures	25-26	8-9 weeks
Amazon Parrots	26-28	8-10 weeks
Lories	23-27	8-12 weeks
(shorter periods in the smaller Australian species which are not available)		
Grey Parrots	28	12 weeks
Poicephalus (Senegal, etc) Parrots	26-28	11-12 weeks
Eclectus Parrots	28	11 weeks

not cause them to desert and will enable the breeder to follow closely the breeding cycle and possibly rectify anything that goes wrong. Initially, it will be possible to discover if the eggs are fertile. Infertile eggs are light in weight and appearance and usually have glossy shells. In fertile eggs held up to a strong light after about 6 days' incubation, the first signs of development – a few thin lines – can be seen. A fertile egg darkens as the chick develops, losing its glossy, new-laid appearance. Table 3 provides a guide to the lengths of incubation and fledging periods in various parrots.

The embryo may die at any stage of the incubation period. The most common causes of death are chilling, due to the egg being left unincubated for a long period, and weakness of the embryo. There are several reasons for the latter but inadequate feeding of the parents, which are therefore unable to pass on all the vital nutrients to the embryo, is a common one. Most upsetting of all is when the chick develops

Figure 36. Candling an egg using a torch and a box. The light shining through the hole in the top of the box will show up the contents of the egg so that you can ascertain whether or not it is fertile. A table lamp can be used instead of a torch.

full-term but fails to penetrate the shell. This is known as dead-in-shell. Often the chick can be heard calling inside the egg; it makes the initial pip but is unable to rotate within the egg to release itself. (An egg tooth on the upper mandible cuts the shell as the chick turns within it.) Again, a weakness in the chick could be to blame for dead-in-shell; alternatively, the chick may be wrongly positioned within the egg, or the shell may be so thick the chick cannot penetrate it.

It is possible to assist chicks to hatch – to save their lives by removing them from the egg. However, the timing is crucial and a beginner is not recommended to attempt this unless advised by an experienced breeder.

Many breeders have been tempted to open eggs which they believe to be overdue. One word covers this situation: don't! There is nothing to be gained and everything to be lost. If the chick is known to be overdue and can be heard inside this is a different matter – but inexperienced breeders may be tempted to open an egg without knowing the stage of incubation it has reached – perhaps when the other eggs in the clutch are overdue, or thought to be so. The incubation period is variable and can be influenced by external conditions. Also, many hens do not commence incubation when the first egg is laid, even although they remain in the box. This means that it is usually impossible to know precisely when incubation commenced. Not until the last egg laid is at least 7 days overdue should eggs be opened and only then if there are no signs of life. Opening eggs will reveal whether they were fertile and at what stage the embryo died. There are so many reasons for eggs failing to hatch that it is only rarely possible to take practical steps to prevent this happening again, but knowledge of the stage at which the egg failed helps to eliminate some possibilities.

Egg-breaking

Another frustrating problem is egg-breaking by the parent birds. This may be due to a habit which is difficult to stop, or the cause could be a calcium deficiency which results in thin-shelled eggs. The latter is easily rectified with Collo-Cal D® (see p.76); the former is difficult to cure. If the male is responsible he will have to be removed while the female is laying and her eggs must then be transferred to another female or to an incubator. Sometimes egg-breaking is accidental and can be prevented by changing the shape of the nest-box from tall to oblong. The birds are then no longer forced to drop down on to the eggs.

Figure 37. Goldie's Lorikeets aged 30 and 32 days.

Figure 38. Grey Parrot chick aged 4 weeks.

CHICKS

When the chicks hatch, nest inspection should be carried out daily. It may then be possible to prevent the loss of chicks. A common problem is that of parents failing to feed their young. Not all birds feed chicks on the day they hatch, but thereafter it should be noted whether they have full crops; it is not necessary to handle chicks to ascertain this. The crop is the area below the throat and it will bulge out, like a small sack, when the chicks have been fed. If they are not being fed or brooded adequately, and especially if one or more has died, they can, if feasible, be transferred to a pair with chicks of similar age, the same species or closely related. Some species – Redrump Parrakeets are a notable example – will feed almost any parrot species (at least until they grow too large) while other individuals will not accept chicks which are different from their own. One can never predict whether foster chicks will be accepted. The alternative is hand-feeding.

Hand-feeding

It is more difficult to hand-feed very young chicks, partly because of the frequency with which they need feeding and partly because, when very young, chicks cannot survive mistakes in the diet or temperature. Experience of hand-feeding is therefore best gained with chicks which are just starting to feather, rather than those of a very few days old.

The first requirement is accommodation where the temperature can be thermostatically controlled; this can be a still air (not forced air) incubator, a hospital cage or a purpose-built brooder. The latter is simply a wooden box with a glass or Perspex front. It can be heated by two 60 watt bulbs which are controlled by a thermostat. (Aquaria shops sell thermostats suitable for this purpose.) The bulbs can be located in a separate compartment at the side of the brooder or in the roof. There is a risk of overheating the base of the container (a cardboard carton is suitable) holding the chicks if the heat source is under the floor. As a temporary emergency measure a light bulb or angle-poise lamp can be suspended over a box containing the chick or chicks.

Before taking a chick from the nest for hand-feeding it must be realised that this is an extremely time-consuming task. The chick will have to be fed every 2 to 4 hours (or hourly if under about 3 days old) during the day for a period of 2 to 4 months, depending on its age and species.

Before installing the chick in its new accommodation, everything must be prepared: the heated cage or heat pad, a teaspoon adapted for feeding chicks, paper towels and/or pet litter in the form of compressed wood shavings.

The temperature should be pre-set a day in advance to make sure it does not fluctuate. For chicks hatched in an incubator and removed to the brooder, it should be the same as that used for hatching, i.e. about 37° C (99° F). Ideally, two or more thermometers should be used to avoid the possibility of accidents caused by a faulty thermometer.

Chicks of a few days old which have no feathers should be maintained at a temperature of 32-35° C (90-95° F). However, the requirements of individual

Figure 39. Electrically heated brooder for rearing parrot chicks. The base contains two 60 watt bulbs. Note the water container — to maintain sufficient humidity.

chicks should be noted. If a chick is too hot, it may be very restless and panting with its beak open. If there are several chicks and they are widely separated this is usually an indication (in small chicks) that they are too warm. A chick which is cold will appear lethargic and the food will be digested slowly. If chicks of different ages and requirements are kept together, the temperature will be dictated by the youngest chick which requires a warmer temperature. A single chick will usually require a higher temperature than several chicks which cluster together. Large species maintain their body temperature more easily than small ones.

Never handle chicks with cold hands. Either wash your hands in warm water or wrap a piece of tissue or paper towel around the chick. Allow it to stand on a surface such as cloth towelling on which its feet can grip and not slide apart.

Heat the food in the smallest available saucepan together with the feeding implement – a teaspoon with the sides bent slightly inwards. (Some chicks will feed satisfactorily from an ordinary teaspoon.) The modified teaspoon can be used from the time the chick hatches. At no stage is it necessary to use a dropper or a syringe. Any chick will feed readily from a spoon because it can use the normal pumping action which would occur if it was being fed by its parent. It is most important to remember that the spoon and the food must be warm; if a chick fails to feed it is usually because one or both is not warm enough. (Alternatively, the chick may be weak or ailing.) Before feeding, test the first few spoonfuls with the tongue to ensure the temperature is correct. As chicks grow, they will take cooler food but at first they demand it hot.

During feeding, any food which falls on the chick's skin or plumage must be

Figure 40. Chicks removed for hand-rearing, can be fed with a spoon, the sides of which have been bent inwards.

wiped off. A damp paper towel is ideal for this purpose. Chicks must be kept scrupulously clean, especially in the region of the mouth, or infections can occur. A cotton-wool bud can be used to clean inside the mouths of chicks of larger species.

Paper towelling can be used on the floor of the chick's container at first. Later this should be changed to pet-litter (compressed wood shavings). If the latter is used, the chick's mouth must be clean and dry before it is returned to the container otherwise wood shavings can stick to it and the chick might attempt to swallow them. By the time chicks reach weaning age, they should be kept on welded mesh – earlier if there is any suggestion of a foot deformity.

It is difficult to recommend a diet because so many are used with success. For beginners, however, the diet should be simple and easy to prepare. I would suggest human baby foods. For all species for the first few days (and for Lories right up to weaning age) I use tinned foods – pure fruit and bone and beef broth with vegetables in approximately equal proportions, with water added. It is quick and easy to prepare and seems to suit all parrot species, with the exception of Cockatiels, which need ground-up seed added at an early stage.

Various items can be added for the larger parrots as they progress, such as ground-up sunflower seed, and spinach and carrot which have been puréed in a blender.

The two most common mistakes are probably feeding food of a too solid consistency to very young chicks – it must be as runny as milk – and giving an over-rich diet, especially in the early stages. If in doubt, it is better to err on the side of a poor diet as it is much easier to kill a chick by feeding it too well than by undernourishing it.

Weaning

When chicks begin to lose interest in their food, weaning time is approaching. Soaked sunflower seed, spray millet, sweet corn and soft pear are favoured items at this stage. When they start to eat sunflower seed, feed it soaked, not dry, and continue to do this for some weeks after they are independent. At this stage, offer a very wide range of foods, as they are more ready to sample a variety of items and will continue to do so all their adult lives. Weaning must be a gradual process with the number of feeds given daily being reduced over a long period until they are spoon-fed once only, late at night.

CHARACTERISTICS OF HAND-REARED PARROTS

Hand-reared parrots are equally suitable for pets or for breeding. Their tameness in an aviary renders them less susceptible to stress than other birds and less easily disturbed when rearing young. It is a myth that hand-reared parrots do not make good parents but they must be reunited with their own species at an early age if they are to be used for breeding purposes.

Hand-reared birds are noted for their tameness and fearlessness. This is in complete contrast to many parent-reared birds, especially Australian parrakeets, which are usually extremely nervous on leaving the nest. Before they are due to fledge it is advisable to place plenty of branches at the end of the aviary if the flight is 240 cm (8 ft) or longer. Newly fledged young sometimes achieve high speeds in their first flights, hit the wire netting which they fail to see, and injure or kill themselves. This is unlikely to occur if such a precaution is taken.

9

ATTENDING TO SICK BIRDS

The keeper who observes his birds closely, and knows them as individuals, is less likely to suffer losses from disease or accident. He will quickly notice if an individual is not behaving normally – usually a sign that it is sick or injured.

This is more easily observed in birds kept indoors than in those in aviaries. The latter are less tame and more likely to 'tighten up' when approached. An unobserved ailing bird usually has plumage which is ruffled rather than tight, eyes dull and slightly sunken and stands for long periods on two feet with its head tucked into the feathers of the back. Healthy birds, except very young ones, usually rest in this manner on one foot. However, there are some birds which habitually break this rule – which is why it is important to know birds as individuals.

The condition of the droppings also provides a clue to the state of a bird's health. Frequently beginners are worried because they have observed that a bird's droppings are loose. This in itself is not a sign of illness. However, in seed-eating birds such as Budgerigars, which normally have droppings which are firm and not at all watery, loose droppings could well be a sign of illness, unless the birds had suddenly been fed large quantities of green food, in which case loose droppings would be expected. On more than one occasion, parrot-owners have told me that they have ceased to feed fruit to their birds because it makes their droppings loose! This is normal and no reason to withhold fruit.

Occasionally, the droppings can indicate exactly what is wrong with a bird. An example is that of a Hawk-headed Parrot in my collection. She was losing weight and her health was obviously deteriorating. Examination of the droppings revealed small particles of undigested seed. The droppings were abnormally coloured and of a peculiar consistency. I took her to my veterinarian and we perused the pages of a comprehensive veterinary textbook and actually came across photographs of identical droppings, associated with birds suffering from a pancreatic deficiency. The solution was a very simple one: a daily dose of the powder contained within Pancrex X® capsules. Within a very few days, undigested food particles had ceased to appear in the droppings.

Unfortunately, diagnosis is very rarely as simple as that. It must be borne in mind that relatively little is known about the diseases of exotic birds. Diagnosis is difficult, often impossible, while the bird is alive. Even a post-mortem examination will not always reveal the cause of death. Therefore, all that can be done in most cases is to administer heat and a broad-spectrum antibiotic. If the latter is ineffective, sensitivity tests will have to be carried out by a veterinarian or other qualified person to discover to which antibiotic the condition will respond. This will take a day or two, which is one reason why it is important to act immediately illness is recognised.

One sometimes hears it said that it is useless to consult a veterinarian because most have little knowledge of tropical birds. This is entirely the wrong attitude because it results in veterinarians being denied the opportunity to work with them. Many veterinarians are interested in birds and welcome the chance to work with something different. It is worth contacting the secretary of a local cage bird society to enquire whether such a veterinarian is known to its members.

CARE OF SICK BIRDS

A costly mistake which, regrettably, is made by countless beginners and even by those with some experience, is the failure to act quickly when a bird is unwell. The condition of a small bird usually deteriorates very quickly. Sick birds usually stop feeding; without food to maintain their body temperature they cannot survive long and, if the weather is cold, they are unlikely to survive the night. If in doubt about a bird's condition, the maxim should therefore be 'Better safe than sorry'. Place the bird in warm surroundings immediately.

Heat is the most important requirement of most ailing birds and this alone will often effect a recovery. But how is the heat to be supplied? Most beginners are totally unprepared for such an emergency. If they have ever thought about the necessity of supplying heat to a sick bird they may have considered that placing its cage in front of a fire in a warm kitchen will suffice. This is not so. It must be possible either to control the heat supplied by means of a thermostat or to provide a very local source of heat out of which the bird can move if it so desires, and as it begins to feel better. A hospital cage will fulfil the first requirement and an infra-red lamp the second. Hospital cages are best used for small birds in my opinion. Larger species will derive more benefit from an infra-red lamp. Hospital cages can be obtained from the larger avicultural suppliers or from companies which specialise in electrical equipment for the aviculturist. They are expensive but considered against the cost of a bird and the possible means of saving its life, the expense is negligible.

Once the condition of an ailing bird begins to improve, the heat can gradually be diminished. Because of the disparity between the temperature indoors and that outdoors, it is not always possible to return birds to their aviaries during the winter months, or a mild spell has to be awaited to avoid a great contrast in temperature. Therefore, temporary indoor accommodation must not be overlooked because, sooner or later, this will be essential.

In many parrots, the pair bond is so strong that separating them from their mates can cause stress and even depression. Where a strong pair bond exists, it is often advisable to ensure that the mate of a sick bird is within sight and sound (preferably caged by its side) of the patient. If no infectious disease is present, the two birds can be caged together providing an infra-red lamp is used, so that the healthy bird can move out of the heat. This is not advised if a hospital cage is used.

However, it must be remembered that birds which have been in an aviary which are suddenly closely confined may fight under these conditions. Caging side by side is therefore usually preferable.

COMMON COMPLAINTS

Depression

Mention has been made of depression – and let there be no doubt that intelligent birds like parrots can suffer from this. It may be caused by the loss of a mate, in which case a replacement should be found as quickly as possible. As an emergency temporary measure, a bird of a closely-related species can be used as a companion.

Burns

All sorts of mishaps can occur to inquisitive pet birds which spend long periods out of their cages. These include burns. The advice of a leading American veterinarian is that, if the burn is a mild one, it should be sprayed with cold water. On no account should any ointment or grease be applied. Instead the affected area should be treated with an anti-inflammatory powder or spray. Bandaging may be necessary, also antibiotics, and so a veterinarian must be consulted. The bird is likely to show symptoms of stress and must be kept as quiet as possible, and warm. Acid burns should be treated with a thin layer of baking soda mixed with water and alkali burns with vinegar.

Leg injuries

Pet birds occasionally suffer leg injuries. It is advisable to remove, or have a veterinarian remove, the leg ring which is used for identification purposes by breeders or importers. Keep a record of the ring number, if there is one. Many birds have lost a leg due to over-tight rings or by the ring becoming impaled on some spiky object.

If the leg is broken, confine the bird to its cage, remove the perches, do not handle it but take it to a veterinarian. An X-ray may be necessary to determine the correct treatment. The fractured ends must be realigned and held together; a rigid splint may have to be applied. Fractures usually heal in about 4 weeks.

Worms

All species of birds have intestinal parasites, but of those popular with aviculturists, Australian parrakeets and Cockatiels are the most susceptible because they spend a lot of time on the ground. The roundworm *(Ascaridia)* is commonly found in these birds; its eggs are expelled in the birds' droppings and may be picked up by foraging birds, which thus become infected or reinfected. This is one reason why concrete floors are recommended as it is easier to keep them clean: in a turf floor, the eggs can remain present and viable for long periods.

When a beginner buys susceptible species from a breeder he should ask him or her to demonstrate how worming is carried out. Many breeders use a tube to ensure that the worming preparation goes straight into the birds' crop. However, this method often causes stress to the bird – and to the person carrying it out if he or she is not very confident. It is not essential to use a tube. The method I adopt is safer and less stressful.

A widely used anthelmintic, Nilverm® (ICI), obtainable from a veterinarian, should be diluted with nine parts of water. For a bird of the body weight of a Golden-mantled Rosella (about 110 g or 4 oz), 1 ml of the solution should be given. A dropper marked with graduations up to 1 ml (such as that provided with a bottle of Abidec® vitamins) is filled with the mixture which is dripped on to the tongue a little at a time so that the bird is forced to swallow. In about five goes, waiting each time for it to swallow, the appropriate dose is given. Occasionally a bird will vomit some minutes later, but I have never found that this has rendered the treatment ineffective. Worms will be passed from 5 to 20 hours later. Before returning the birds to their aviary, the floor should be scrubbed and disinfected to prevent reinfestation from picking up worm eggs.

10
MAKING THE MOST
OF YOUR HOBBY

In every sphere of life, whether it is business, sport or hobby, those who participate most keenly are the ones who derive most from it. So it is with keeping and breeding birds. A lifetime of this absorbing pastime will teach only a small fraction of the knowledge there is to be gained. Every breeder is a storehouse of information that is not duplicated exactly in any other brain. Unfortunately, much of the knowledge accumulated by every breeder is lost because he or she has not taken the time to record it and subsequently to have it published in a source which will make it readily available to others with similar interests.

This is often because a breeder believes that he cannot possibly contribute anything to the knowledge of a species which has been kept in captivity for perhaps a century or more. Often it is the most common species in captivity about which comparatively little of real value has been recorded, while rare species are written up in minute detail. The beginner with an unbiased eye, to whom everything is new, is just as likely to observe and record something of significant value as is the most experienced aviculturist.

From the start keep thorough records of your birds. Index cards can be used to record details of individual birds, especially those relating to breeding, and a large record book can be used to note birds bought and sold, to keep an annual stock inventory and, most important, to detail quirks of behaviour which would almost certainly be forgotten or incompletely recalled unless recorded on the spot. Such information is not only invaluable for personal reference, it can form the basis for articles.

Every level of journal exists, from the typewritten newsletter of the local club to the more professional quarterly or bi-monthly magazine of specialist societies which have members all over the country and in many countries throughout the world. Most find it difficult to fill their magazines and welcome contributions of a practical nature.

The societies which produce the magazines are the primary means of bringing together people with similar interests. Meeting people with the same aims increases the enjoyment gained from any hobby; on a practical level, it results in sources for selling surplus stock and of obtaining new birds. Sale and exchange is effected through advertisements in club journals, as well as through the weekly magazine *Cage and Aviary Birds*. Without the magazines, aviculture would be carried out on a more local basis, rather than having the countrywide exchange of stock which presently exists and it would be more difficult to obtain the rarer species.

Specialist and other avicultural societies can get together to help to fight the legislation which places increasing restrictions on aviculture and bird-keeping. Only strongly supported societies, representing the majority of those who keep birds, are likely to be effective in combating the introduction of detrimental legislation.

Not everyone takes a sympathetic attitude towards bird-keepers – but they are more likely to do so if aviculture is seen to be contributing to scientific knowledge. It is not only those who breed birds or record details of their behaviour who can do this. The bodies of birds of non-domesticated species are of great value to natural history museums – but all too often birds that die are 'wasted' because no use is made of their remains. All bird-keepers should contact their nearest natural history museum or the most important collection in the country – that of the British Museum (Natural History), Tring, Herts, HP23 6AP, and enquire whether the collection could use the bodies of birds or their chicks, also eggs. Even birds in poor feather condition are useful to those museums which have skeleton collections. It should also be noted that those on which post-mortem examinations have been carried out can be used – but the person carrying out the autopsy should be advised beforehand of the eventual destination of the material. It is satisfying to know that a bird which, perhaps, one has bred can be presented to a museum so that it has not lived in vain and will be a useful source of reference for many years to come.

Those who indulge in bird-keeping should not look upon it merely as a pleasant hobby but should consider how they can make a contribution to science. It may be a small contribution: this does not matter. It is the accumulation of knowledge which is so important.

USEFUL ADDRESSES

United Kingdom

John E. Haith, Park Street, Cleethorpes, South Humberside DN35 7NF. (Suppliers of seeds and various foods)

A.C. Hughes, 1 High Street, Hampton Hill, Middlesex. (Rings)

G.H. McCreery & Sons, Carr Lane, Shipley, Yorkshire. (Rings)

National Council of Aviculture, Sec. J.A.W. Prior, 103 Horncastle Road, Lee, London SE12.

Ponderosa Aviaries, The White House, Branch Lane, The Reddings, Cheltenham, Gloucestershire. (Books and avicultural supplies)

Porters, 81 Plashet Grove, London E6. (Cages and all avicultural equipment)

United States of America

A-E Leg Bands, P.O. Box 523, Miami, Florida. (Rings)

Audubon Publishing Co., 3449 N. Western Avenue, Chicago, ILL 60618. (Books)

Bird Band International, 10441 Barbara Ann, Cypress, CA 90630. (Rings)

Kellogg Inc., 322 East Florida St, Milwaukee, WI 53201. (Seeds and foods)

REFERENCES

BOOKS

Forshaw, J.M. (1973) *Parrots of the World* Lansdowne Press, Sydney, Australia.

Hayward, J. (1979) *Lovebirds and Their Colour Mutations* Blandford Press, Poole, Dorset, UK.

Low, R. (1977) *Lories and Lorikeets* Paul Elek, London, UK.

Low, R. (1980) *Parrots, Their Care and Breeding* Blandford Press, Poole, Dorset, UK.

Low, R. (1984) *Endangered Parrots* Blandford Press, Poole, Dorset, UK.

Pearce, D.W. (1983) *Aviary Design & Construction* Pet Handbook Series, Blandford Press, Poole, Dorset, UK.

Smith, G.A. (1978) *Encyclopedia of Cockatiels* T.F.H. Publications, New Jersey, USA.

PERIODICALS

United Kingdom

Avicultural Magazine (Quarterly. The Avicultural Society, Windsor Forest Stud, Mill Ride, Ascot, Berkshire)

Cage and Aviary Birds (Weekly. Surrey House, 1 Throwley Way, Sutton, Surrey)

Magazine of the Parrot Society (Monthly. 19a De Parys Ave, Bedford, Bedfordshire)

United States of America

Agapornis World (Monthly. African Love Bird Society, 2336 Cherimoya, Vista, CA 92083)

American Cage-Bird Magazine (Monthly. 3449 N. Western Avenue, Chicago, ILL 60618)

Avicultural Bulletin (Monthly. Avicultural Society of America, P.O. Box 157, Stanton, CA 92083)

Watchbird (Bi-monthly. American Federation of Aviculture, P.O. Box 1568, Redondo Beach, CA 90278)

INDEX

Numbers in *italics* refer to illustrations.